My Little French Kitchen

Over 100 recipes from the mountains, market
squares and shores of France

With photography by David Loftus and illustrations by Rachel Khoo

MICHAEL JOSEPH
an imprint of Penguin Books

Published by the Penguin Group

Penguin Books Ltd, 80 Strand, London WC2R 0RL, England

Penguin Group (USA) Inc., 375 Hudson Street, New York, New York 10014, USA

Penguin Group (Canada), 90 Eglinton Avenue East, Suite 700, Toronto, Ontario, Canada M4P 2Y3
(a division of Pearson Penguin Canada Inc.)

Penguin Ireland, 25 St Stephen's Green, Dublin 2, Ireland (a division of Penguin Books Ltd)

Penguin Group (Australia), 707 Collins Street, Melbourne, Victoria 3008, Australia
(a division of Pearson Australia Group Pty Ltd)

Penguin Books India Pvt Ltd, 11 Community Centre,
Panchsheel Park, New Delhi – 110 017, India

Penguin Group (NZ), 67 Apollo Drive, Rosedale, Auckland 0632, New Zealand
(a division of Pearson New Zealand Ltd)

Penguin Books (South Africa) (Pty) Ltd, Block D, Rosebank Office Park,
181 Jan Smuts Avenue, Parktown North, Gauteng 2193, South Africa

Penguin Books Ltd, Registered Offices: 80 Strand, London WC2R 0RL, England

www.penguin.com

First published 2013
001

Typeset in Arial and Plebeya

Colour Reproduction by Tag: response
Printed in Italy by Graphicom srl

A CIP catalogue record for this book is available from the British Library

ISBN: 978–0–718–17747–8

After the whirlwind months that followed the release of *The Little Paris Kitchen* book and television show, my life seemed to go back to normal. I was still living in the same apartment with my kitchenette composed of two gas rings and a mini oven, still no dishwasher in sight. I bought my grocery shopping from the same fruit and veg guy, visited the same baker and traipsed to my butcher. Little had changed. Aside from my cheese lady's persistent jokey questioning, 'Where are the cameras?', each time I picked up a hunk of fruity Comté, life went on in my little kitchen as before. But I could feel a growing rumble in my stomach, and it wasn't because I was craving a piece of French cheese and crusty baguette, my all-time favourite snack.

Just like when I moved from London to Paris eight years ago, I had an itchy yearning for new tastes and discoveries. I still loved Paris (I always will), but I felt I wanted to charter unknown territories in the country I had called home for almost a decade. It was time for me to pack up my cooking kit and discover what lay beyond the twenty *arrondisements* that piece Paris together.

Deciding where to go was easier said than done. When it comes to culinary culture and history, France is as rich and dense as my chocolate beret cake (see page 130). My friends asked, 'How are you going to visit the whole of France and write about all the food? *Ce n'est pas possible!*' Most of them thought I had bitten off more than I could chew, and I can chew a lot! France has a gastronomic wealth that has been documented painstakingly by many other chefs and Francophile food writers throughout the centuries, from Marie-Antoine Carême and Auguste Escoffier to Elizabeth David and Jane Grigson.

This book took me on an adventure around France by train, plane, bus, car and bike – at one point, I was even driving a minibus. Up winding roads and down dirt tracks, through howling wind, rain *comme les vaches pissent* (like cows peeing, as the French say), snow, hail . . . you name it, I braved every kind of weather. I was a woman on a mission to discover those recipes, now long forgotten and stuffed in the back of a drawer, made by regional French grandmas. But not just the old recipes: I was interested to see what France looked like today. How was the younger generation eating? Paris, being the capital, is a Mecca for new concepts and trends, but I was impressed to see that a movement of young food producers can also be found all over the country, combining old traditions with their new ideas.

France's artisanal food scene, in common with other countries in the western world, is fighting against the big food corporations. Although France has always prided itself on its strong culinary heritage, as I visited producers, farmers and local shops it became evident that all is not as rosy as one might think. There are battles against environmental changes and government regulations, combined with the lack of a new generation to take over traditional roles and a sharp rise in production costs. But, despite all these challenges, the passion and hard work that goes into creating products to sell with pride shines through brightly in the end result.

After each of my voyages, I would return with my suitcase laden with random bits and bobs I had picked up, from edible souvenirs like special dried herbs and lavender honey, to cheese paper wrappers or the odd funny looking spoon. In my little kitchen in Paris, the tasty trinkets would be turned into dishes to eat with friends and family. Each meal tells the story of my trip, allowing me to share my edible exploration and the complexities and oddities of each region's food culture.

My travels took me took me to many places all across this wonderful country, from Biarritz, the surfers' paradise, with its fiery Espelette pepper and Basque kisses, to the elegant chateaux and rickety, but utterly charming, oyster shacks in the Bordeaux region. I fell in love with the Christmas sparkle and spice of the Alsacian winter markets, and Brittany with its iconic lighthouses dotting the coast and its delicious giant blue lobsters. And I marvelled at the almighty Lyon with its snowcapped mountains and warming dishes, which contrasted with the bright colours in the vegetable dishes of Provence that radiated summer heat.

And so this book is not about the whole of France – even a multi-volume epic couldn't hope to do justice to that idea – but it is about the trips I made around French villages and towns, the people who welcomed me into their homes, farms and food shops and all the little culinary quirks that I stumbled upon. Each recipe is a postcard from my little kitchen to yours, savouring the flavours, smells and textures that inspired me, and that I hope will inspire you too. *Bon voyage* on my little culinary tour of France! I hope you enjoy the trip.

Rachel

Brittany

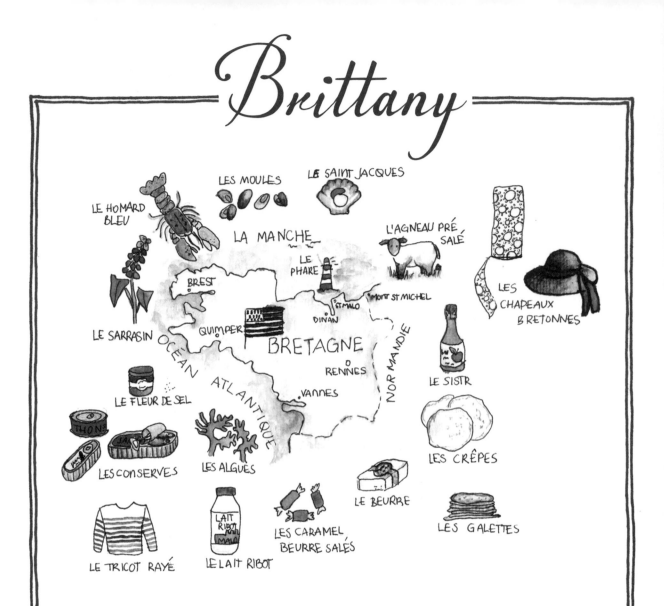

LE SAINT JACQUES

LES MOULES

LE HOMARD BLEU

LA MANCHE

L'AGNEAU PRÉ SALÉ

LE PHARE

LES CHAPEAUX BRETONNES

BREST

ST MALO

MONT ST MICHEL

LE SARRASIN

OCEAN ATLANTIQUE

QUIMPER

DINAN

BRETAGNE

NORMANDIE

LE SISTR

LE FLEUR DE SEL

RENNES

VANNES

THON

LES CONSERVES

LES ALGUES

LES CRÊPES

LE BEURRE

LE TRICOT RAYÉ

LAIT RIBOT MALO

LE LAIT RIBOT

LES CARAMEL BEURRE SALÉS

LES GALETTES

BLUE AND WHITE STRIPES, BUTTERY DELIGHTS AND COASTAL COOKING

Le crachin, as the Bretons refer to the so-called 'spitting rain', was almost constant when I visited the region in the early months of the year. The persistent drizzle wasn't the only thing that was like home: the lush green pastures, neatly trimmed hedges and pretty stone country cottages reminded me of the verdant British landscape around where I grew up in Berkshire. It is easy to see how Brittany acquired the nickname 'Little Britain'.

Brittany is one of France's most iconic regions, being the home of many of the country's most popular foodstuffs, as well as the sartorial export of blue and white stripes. Butter, *galettes*, *crêpes*, caramel, *fleur de sel*, dairy and all its derivatives are entrenched in the food culture.

Thanks to this abundance of dairy produce and other such delights, Brittany is one of the best places in France to have breakfast. French breakfasts are often an afterthought, usually consisting of a cup of black coffee and a flaky croissant at best, and toasted leftover baguette at worst. However, I enjoyed some exemplary homemade breakfasts during my stays at various B&Bs around the region, including homemade jams and breads as well as the thickest, creamiest homemade yoghurt, which inspired my recipe on page 53. One of the most epic versions featured the legendary golden, caramelized *kouign-amann* (see page 42), Brittany's greatest pastry.

Now, *crêpes* and *galettes* were nothing new to me: Paris has a *crêperie* on every corner and around the Montparnasse area there are plenty of Breton *crêperies*. However, what I found rather intriguing was what they filled their buckwheat pancakes with. Not the usual egg and cheese, but a grilled, quite spicy (for the French) sausage. Simply popped whole into the middle of each *galette*, then wrapped tightly to make a sort of *galette* hot dog. At the morning markets of Dinan and Rennes, this unlikely breakfast treat was *de rigeur* from the various food trucks sandwiched between produce sellers.

Markets are among Brittany's highlights. The *Marché des Lices* on Saturdays in the centre of Rennes is probably one of the best I've been to in France. Unlike most Parisian markets, where the selection is excellent but resellers, not farmers, operate most stands, in Rennes the producers themselves run the majority. Being in a coastal corner of France, the choice of seafood is out of this world. I have never seen such big lobsters, oysters in every size and shape possible, cockles, clams, razor clams, mussels, scallops and fish fresh off the boat, glistening on ice.

More secrets were discovered on a trip to Saint-Malo, the beautiful town on the coast set within a medieval wall. Down a cobbled street I found the king of butter, Yves Bordier, with his renowned boutique and restaurant, complete with butter museum. Bretons love their butter and Yves Bordier reigns supreme on the menus of the finest restaurants in France and abroad. His butter looks like little yellow bricks flecked with sea salt, seaweed, smoked salt or even yuzu.

The rugged beauty of Brittany's coast is awe-inspiring. Lighthouses pop up on rocky cliffs with stretches of sandy beaches sandwiched inbetween. Cap Fréhel lies on one such cliff, with its majestic green-tipped beacon in a protected nature reserve. Small rocks jut out of the wet sand at low tide, revealing wild mussels and seaweed. The salt in the air has you licking your lips, stirring up an appetite for a picnic or some cooking on the beach (see page 24).

Sea salt is big business in Brittany but also a very time-consuming one. It is carefully harvested mainly around Guérande, the southwestern corner of Brittany where they produce the famous *fleur de sel*, a sea salt prized by chefs and food enthusiasts. Salt is harvested in the summer months, but requires meticulous attention throughout the year in preparation, as well as a great deal of *savoir faire* adapting to the whims of the weather at any time. Clay walls are built and maintained inside ponds, for the salt water to be ushered though, and it is eventually raked into piles to dry. The *fleur de sel* are the delicate crystals that develop on the top of the water and they are pulled aside.

From the knob of butter that sizzles in the pan to the understated sprinkle of salt that brings an entire dish together, the gastronomy of Brittany may not have sophisticated Parisian glamour, but it is responsible for produce that is fundamental to dishes created in renowned restaurants around the world. From moist sea bass baked in a salt crust, buttermilk lamb or choux pastry lighthouses with butter caramel sauce (see pages 16, 30 and 46), the recipes in this chapter draw their inspiration from those little touches and apply them to dishes that can be cooked in any kitchen (whether home or Michelin-starred). I hope you fall for the food of Brittany as much as I did.

Huîtres grillées en persillade

OYSTERS GRILLED WITH PARSLEY CRUMBS

I love the purity of a just-shucked oyster, either as it comes or with a simple squeeze of lemon. But when they are in such abundance, as they are in Cancale and other parts of Brittany, you might as well experiment with different flavours. The crunchy texture of the breadcrumbs highlights the smoothness of the oyster flesh, providing a playful and delicious contrast.

Makes 12
Preparation time: 10 minutes
Cooking time: 10 minutes

2 level tbsp butter

2 cloves of garlic, peeled and finely minced

4 tbsp white breadcrumbs (made from stale bread)

4 tbsp finely chopped fresh flat-leaf parsley

12 oysters, shucked (see page 58)

wedges of lemon, to serve

Heat a frying pan over a medium heat. Add the butter and garlic. Once the butter is melted and the garlic slightly softened, add the breadcrumbs, stirring every so often until light golden. Place in a bowl and toss with the parsley.

Preheat the grill to high. Remove any excess juices from your shucked oysters. Place the oysters on a tray that will hold them upright (madeleine or muffin tins work well) and grill for 2–3 minutes. Sprinkle over the breadcrumb mixture and serve with the lemon wedges.

Une petite astuce – tip If you don't have a madeleine or muffin tray, make a bed out of rock salt on a baking tray and nestle the oysters in it (see page 59).

Faire en avance – get ahead The parsley breadcrumbs can be made in advance and stored in an airtight container for a couple of days.

Un-shucked oysters will keep for about two days. Check with your fishmonger.

Court bouillon Breton

BRITTANY BOUILLON

Forget salty stock cubes and their powdered counterparts – in Brittany, sachets of gourmet bouillon are *de rigeur*. Made using the locally available seaweed it gives an extra angle to this essential store-cupboard ingredient. Try adding to soups, sprinkling on salads or popping into a stew for a taste of *Bretagne*. This is a great recipe for making your own bouillon.

Makes approx. 30g
Preparation time: 20 minutes
Cooking time: 3–4 hours
Resting time: overnight

2 carrots, peeled

2 sticks of celery (ideally with leaves), remove the long strings from the celery

2 leeks, trimmed and washed

10 mushrooms, brushed

1 clove of garlic, peeled

1 tsp coarse sea salt

10g dried seaweed

Preheat the oven to 110°C. Use a speed peeler or vegetable peeler to make thin ribbons of carrot. Finely slice the celery (or, very carefully, use a mandolin with the guard). Pull apart the layers of the leek. Finely slice the mushrooms and garlic. Try to make all the vegetables an even thickness so that they take the same amount of time to cook.

Lay all the vegetables flat on parchment paper and arrange the celery leaves among the vegetables. Place the parchment paper directly on the oven rack and cook for 3–4 hours or until the vegetables lose their moisture and crisp up. Turn off the heat and leave them to dry out overnight in the oven with the door ajar.

Blitz the vegetables with the salt and seaweed in a food processor. Keep in an airtight container in a cool dark place.

Les petites astuces – tips Make your own bouillon 'teabags' for a quick cup of soup. Cut out six squares of muslin, each approximately 8cm x 8cm. Place 1 tablespoon of the mixture in the centre of each muslin square. Gather the corners together and twist the ends tightly. Use a length of thread to secure the bag in a tight knot or tie with string; leave a long bit of thread for dunking. Repeat with the rest of the muslin squares.

Daurade en croûte de sel

HERBY SALT CRUST BREAM

Baking in a salt crust is possibly one of the most effective ways of cooking whole fish. Not only does unveiling the flesh from under a firm cast of salt at the dinner table look pretty classy, but it also traps all the moisture in the flesh while delicately seasoning it.

Serves 4
Preparation time: 10 minutes
Cooking time: 20 minutes

1 lemon

1.5kg coarse sea salt

2 x 450g sea bream or sea bass, gutted and washed

a bunch of fresh sorrel or flat-leaf parsley (approx. 20g)

2 egg whites

steamed new potatoes, tossed in butter, to serve

Preheat the oven to 200°C. Line a baking tray with baking paper.

Zest the lemon into a large bowl and mix with the salt. Cut the lemon into 4 wedges or slices and stuff 2 into the cavity of each fish, along with a couple of leaves of sorrel. Chop up the rest of the sorrel and set aside a couple of tablespoons for garnish. Mix the rest into the lemony salt, then mix in the egg whites. Spread half of the salt mixture over the lined baking tray. Lay the fish on top (with a couple of fingers' space between each piece). Cover the fish with the rest of the salt and bake in the oven for 20 minutes.

When the fish is cooked, remove from the oven and use a knife to crack the crust and gently peel off the salt. Serve the fish with steamed new potatoes tossed in a little butter with the reserved sorrel.

Une petite astuce – tip Make sure to use coarse sea salt as fine sea salt will dissolve in the egg white and won't form a solid crust.

Millefeuilles aux tomates et lentilles

TOMATO AND LENTIL MILLEFEUILLES

You can't visit Brittany or Normandy and not eat a sweet *crêpe* or a savoury *galette*. They are what *choucroute* is to the Alsacians; *pintxos* are to the Basques (see pages 104–9) and *quenelles* to the Lyonnais (see page 184). They are an integral part of the eating culture and best enjoyed with a bottle of the locally produced cider. Breton galettes are always savoury and are always made from buckwheat. Grown since the fifteenth century, buckwheat thrives here and Le Blé Noir de Bretagne is even protected from imposters with its own I.G.P. certificate.

Serves 6
Preparation time: 40 minutes
Resting time: 1 hour, or overnight
Cooking time: 40 minutes

200g buckwheat flour

salt and freshly ground pepper

600ml cold water

vegetable oil, for frying

100g Puy or beluga lentils

1 large courgette, chopped into 3mm cubes

2 red peppers, deseeded and chopped into 3mm cubes

200g cherry tomatoes, finely chopped

1 red onion, peeled and finely chopped

1 tbsp olive oil, plus a little extra for drizzling

300g assorted tomatoes

1 tbsp lemon thyme

Mix the flour and a pinch of salt in a bowl. Make a well in the centre and gradually mix in the water, adding just enough for the batter to have the consistency of double cream. Don't over-mix, as this will produce rubbery galettes. Chill in the fridge for at least an hour, or overnight. Before using, whisk again and add more water if necessary.

Heat a 15–18cm non-stick crêpe pan or a small frying pan over a medium heat and brush with a little vegetable oil. Pour in a small ladleful of the batter and quickly swirl the pan so that the batter coats the base entirely. Cook for 1–2 minutes, loosen around the edge with a spatula, then turn it over and cook for a further minute. Slide the galette out of the pan, then repeat to make 12 galettes, greasing the pan with a little oil each time. Stack the galettes with layers of kitchen towel or baking paper between each one.

Cook the lentils in boiling salted water according to the packet instructions. Drain and mix together with the courgette, peppers, cherry tomatoes, onion and olive oil. Season, to taste, with salt and pepper.

Preheat the oven to 180°C. Line a loose-bottom round baking tin (the size of the galettes) with baking paper. Place one galette at the bottom of the tin. Spread with some of the lentil mixture then top with another galette. Repeat until you have used up all the galettes (finishing with a galette).

Slice the mixed tomatoes and pack them in tightly on top of the galettes. Drizzle with a little olive oil and sprinkle with the thyme. Cook in the oven for 20 minutes. Eat while still hot from the oven.

Les sardines rapides au vinaigre

QUICK PICKLED SARDINES

Shiny silver sardines from Brittany are rather renowned in the Breton markets. Up against the strong tides of the Quiberon Peninsula, the fish have a firmer flesh compared to their southern-European cousins. As a means of preserving their abundant catches, the Quiberonnaise have a long-standing tradition of cooking these little fish and preserving them under a layer of salted butter. An industry grew out of this and you'll find many small factories preserving the local product in dinky tins. This kind of preservation 'en boite' tastes best when it's had at least a couple of days for the flavours to develop. This recipe is quite the opposite: too long in the fridge and you'll be left with sardine mush on your hands, making it perfect for those who are a little impatient.

Serves 5 or 6 as a starter
Preparation time: 10 minutes
Resting time: 6 hours, or overnight

150ml cider vinegar

150ml white wine vinegar

100g sugar

2 tsp table salt

2 bay leaves

10 black peppercorns

2 juniper berries

20 fresh sardine fillets, deboned

1 small cucumber (such as a Lebanese cucumber), sliced into very thin rounds

1 small red onion, peeled and finely sliced

1 lemon, zested and cut into wedges

Place all the ingredients apart from the sardines, cucumber, onion and lemon zest in a pot. Bring to the boil and stir until all the sugar has dissolved. Remove from the heat and leave to cool.

When the brine has cooled to room temperature, pour it into shallow non-metallic dish. Add the sardine fillets (check for bones), cucumber, onion and lemon zest. Make sure everything is submerged in the liquid. Cover the dish in cling film (not foil) and leave in the fridge for at least 6 hours, or overnight.

Serve on buttered rye bread or apple and caraway crackers (see page 234) with wedges of lemon.

Les petites astuces – tips Ask your fishmonger to fillet your sardines for you, as it is a fiddly process.

Don't forget your sardines in the fridge! If they are kept too long in the pickling liquid they will turn mushy after about 24 hours.

Pâtes à la marinière au calvados

CLAM PASTA WITH CALVADOS CREAM

While in Brittany, I had the pleasure of meeting a dynamic young fellow, David Le Ruyet, who is on a one-man mission to make an impact on the local food scene. David grows his own wheat, mills it and then makes pasta, which he sells throughout France and beyond. Due to the weather conditions of the region, David works with the local wheat flour (*blé tendre*) rather than the traditional durum wheat used in pasta making.

In France they have many types of clam, but in the UK cockles are more commonly available and they are virtually the same beast. Their differences are found in their size, and the shape and direction of the ridges on their shells. *Palourdes* (carpet shell clams) are bigger, and therefore plumper and slightly juicier, but cockles are lovely little things, and much more economical, so don't let their posh counterparts sway you away.

Serves 4
Preparation time: 15 minutes
Cooking time: 15 minutes

250g fettuccine, or pasta shapes such as fusilli or conchiglie

1 onion, peeled and finely chopped

1 tbsp butter

150ml calvados

2.5kg clams or cockles, or a mix, scrubbed, broken ones discarded

4 tbsp full-fat crème fraîche

125g mange tout or peas

4 medium fresh sorrel leaves (or a handful of fresh parsley), finely chopped

½ a lemon, zested and cut into wedges

Cook the pasta according to the packet instructions and then drain well through a colander.

In a second large pot cook the onion in the butter until soft and translucent. Add the calvados followed by the clams. Cover with the lid and cook for 2 minutes. Stir, cover with the lid and cook for a further 2–4 minutes; the clams should open up once cooked. If using cockles, cook them for just 2 minutes. Strain the clams through a colander placed over a bowl to catch the liquid and discard any that remain closed.

Return the drained pasta to its pan. Add 4 tablespoons of the strained clam cooking liquid and toss together along with the clams, onions, crème fraîche, mange tout, sorrel leaves and lemon zest. Serve with lemon wedges on the side.

Une petite astuce – tip If serving for a dinner party, shell some of the clams and toss them through the pasta before dividing between bowls. Divide the remaining clams in their shells between the bowls.

Moules aux pommes et calvados

APPLE AND CALVADOS POTTED MUSSELS

The Breton coastline boasts a particularly pretty lighthouse with a watch room painted a vibrant green. Along the spotless sandy beaches at the foot of this lighthouse are jagged grey rocks sticking out of the sand, and clinging to them are thousands of mussels. When I was there, a few locals were making the most of the bounty, picking them off the rocks and smuggling them into bags. Back in my Paris kitchen I decided to combine mussels with some of the other produce from Normandy and Brittany: butter and calvados, which worked a treat.

Serves 4
Preparation time: 20 minutes
Cooking time: 20 minutes
Resting time: at least 1 hour
Equipment: 4 x 200ml glasses or ramekins

200g butter, softened

1kg mussels

50ml calvados

1 shallot, peeled and finely chopped

1 small apple (approx. 100g), chopped into 2mm cubes

salt

a generous pinch of ground white pepper

2 tbsp finely chopped fresh flat-leaf parsley

Place the butter in a small saucepan and melt over a gentle heat. Once melted, set aside. De-beard and scrub the mussels. Clean them and rinse well under cold running water. Discard any broken or open mussels (tap them on a hard surface to see if they close).

Pour the calvados into a large pot and when it begins to steam, throw in the mussels and cover with the lid. Shake the pan from time to time. After 5 minutes all the mussels should have opened up. Leave to cool slightly, before removing them from their shells and setting to one side. Discard the empty shells and any mussels that are still closed.

Using a slotted spoon, remove the milk solids from the butter (the white foam on top) or strain through a small sieve, and skim off any frothy foam.

In a large frying pan fry the shallot and apple in a couple of tablespoons of the clarified butter until the shallot is translucent. Tip in all the mussels and gently warm through for a couple of minutes before removing from the heat. Taste for seasoning; add salt, if required, and the white pepper, and then stir in the parsley.

Divide between the ramekins and pour the remaining butter over the top. Leave to cool before refrigerating. The mussels taste best when they've had a little time for the flavours to develop, but if you really can't wait simply chill until the butter has set to room temperature. Consume within two days.

Agneau au lait ribot avec sarrasin et salade d'herbe

BUTTERMILK LAMB WITH TOASTED BUCKWHEAT AND HERB SALAD

Fourth generation specialist farmer Yannick Frain is, what you might call, the ambassador of the Mouton Prés-Salés – the French equivalent of our salt marsh lamb – and his sheep (mostly black-faced Suffolk) live in the shadow of Mont Saint-Michel. This positioning not only provides a highly impressive backdrop, but also, when the tide is up during the full moon, the marshes are submerged in salt water. Grazing on this grass, rich in some 70 different varieties of plants, imparts a unique flavour to the meat.

Serves 4–6

Preparation time: 20 minutes
Resting time: overnight–2 days
Cooking time: 4 hours

1.2kg lean leg of lamb

200g buttermilk

salt and freshly ground pepper

a knob of butter, for greasing

For the salad

400g buckwheat

a large bunch of fresh mint (approx. 40g)

a large bunch of fresh flat-leaf parsley (approx. 40g)

juice of 1 lemon

4 tbsp olive oil

For the yoghurt sauce

zest and juice of ½ a lemon

600g plain yoghurt

1 red onion, peeled and finely chopped

a pinch of sugar

Place the lamb in a large freezer bag, coating it with the buttermilk, and fasten securely. Leave in the fridge to marinate overnight or preferably for 24–48 hours.

Preheat the oven to 160°C. Place the lamb with the buttermilk, plus 200ml of water, in a deep casserole dish. Season with plenty of salt and pepper. Cook the lamb in the oven for 3½ hours, basting it every hour or so with the cooking liquid. When done, remove from the oven and cover with lightly greased foil to rest for 10 minutes.

For the salad, tip the buckwheat into a large saucepan and dry-toast for about 5 minutes, until it is golden brown and has a nutty fragrance. Remove from the heat and leave to cool. Tear the mint and parsley leaves into the buckwheat, add a pinch of salt, the lemon juice and oil. Toss together then set aside.

To make the yoghurt sauce, mix the lemon zest and juice with the yoghurt, onion and sugar. Season, to taste. To serve, flake the meat and serve on top of the buckwheat with the yoghurt sauce drizzled over.

Sablés aux fromage et tomates

CHEESE AND TOMATO BUTTERY BISCUITS

I have a confession to make: I have a soft spot for those tiny pizza-flavoured crackers you find in France. I was enjoying an aperitif in Brittany when I was offered a small plate of them, which I quickly polished off and began considering a home-baked version. *Sablé* (meaning 'sandy') is quite simply a very buttery biscuit, and shops selling different versions of the *Sablé Breton* are as common as crêperies in the region. They are a poshed-up, yet easy-to-make version of the tiny pizza aperitif crackers you can buy at the supermarket.

Makes 50
Preparation time: 20 minutes
Resting time: 30 minutes
Cooking time: 10 minutes

150g plain white flour

125g cold butter, cut into small cubes

125g finely grated mature Tomme de vâche or other strongly flavoured hard cheese

200g cherry tomatoes, sliced

1–2 tbsp fresh oregano

Mix together the flour, butter and cheese. Rub the fat into the flour between your fingertips until you have a sandy texture then start squashing it together to make it a ball. Wrap the ball of dough in cling film and then roll into a sausage shape, about 3cm in diameter. Chill in the fridge for at least 30 minutes.

Preheat the oven to 180°C. Line a baking tray with baking paper.

Remove the dough from the fridge, peel off the cling film and slice the dough into 3mm rounds. Place the rounds on the lined baking tray, topping each one with a slice of tomato and a pinch of oregano. Bake for 10 minutes or until golden on the bottom. Cool on a rack.

Les petites astuces – tips Be careful as the *sablés* will be very fragile when they come out of the oven.

The tomatoes can be replaced with slices of olives or little pieces of anchovy.

Faire en avance – get ahead The dough can be wrapped and then frozen. Simply slice it and cook from frozen. Will also keep for up to a week in an airtight container in the fridge.

Soupe de homard, lait ribot et fenouil

LOBSTER, FENNEL AND BUTTERMILK SOUP

The lobsters I spotted at the Saturday morning market in Rennes looked more like the deep-sea monsters you imagine as a kid. I have never seen lobsters quite so big and in such abundance. I can only imagine that the Bretons feel that these beautiful lobsters are simply too good to be sent away from their region. Fair play, I say; if I were a local I would agree!

Lobster is a rare treat and not something I eat or cook very often, so when I do, I keep cooking to a minimum so that the flavours can shine through and I make sure to extract as much flavour as possible from the shell.

Serves 4
Preparation time: 20 minutes
Cooking time: 1¼ hours

1 cooked lobster (approx. 1kg) or
4 lobster tails

1 head of fennel

2 lemons

2 tbsp butter

1 onion, peeled and roughly chopped

2 bay leaves

10 black peppercorns

250ml white wine

1 litre water

250ml buttermilk

salt

optional: lobster roe

Carefully remove the lobster meat from the shell or ask your fishmonger to cut it in half to make it easier. Place the meat in a bowl, cover with cling film and leave in the fridge until needed.

Cut the fennel in half lengthways. Chop one half roughly and set aside to use in the stock. Finely slice the other half, discarding the tough stem. Toss in the juice of half a lemon and place in the fridge. Save the green sprigs to use as a garnish.

Place a large pot over a medium heat and add the butter, roughly chopped fennel, onion, bay leaves, the zest from 1 lemon, the lobster shells and peppercorns. Cook, stirring, until the onion is translucent. Add the wine, increase the heat to high and simmer hard for 2 minutes before adding the water. Cover with the lid and leave to simmer gently for 30 minutes. Do not allow it to boil.

Pour the stock through a fine sieve into a large bowl. Press every-thing through the sieve to get the most out of the tasty stock. Discard the solids. Return the stock to the pan and bring to a simmer. Simmer for a 30 minutes, uncovered.

Remove the lobster from the fridge 30 minutes before serving. Add the buttermilk to the stock with a squeeze of lemon; the buttermilk will solidify into clusters. Season to taste.

Divide the lobster meat between serving bowls, pour the soup over the top and add the finely sliced fennel, the zest from 1 lemon, any fennel sprigs and the lobster roe, if using. Serve with lemon wedges on the side.

Paupiette au poulet, chataigne et pomme avec salade de chou-rave

ROASTED CHICKEN PARCELS WITH KOHLRABI SLAW

With apple orchards being a fixture of the agricultural landscape of Brittany and Normandy, it is no surprise the drink of choice is cider and, for those wanting to put a little hair on their chest, calvados. I tasted a surprising cider from Sacha Crommar, who is part of a local group of producers experimenting with and refining traditional techniques in the region. To make his Cidre Chataigne, the pressed juice is fermented with chestnuts, adding an earthy complexity to the flavour. That combination of tastes inspired this dish; perfect for a lazy Sunday lunch and easily prepared in advance – the chicken can be stuffed and kept in the fridge, covered, for up to 48 hours.

Serves 4

Preparation time: 30 minutes
Cooking time: 45 minutes

4 large deboned chicken thighs, skin on

salt and freshly ground pepper

3 shallots, peeled

1 small apple, cut into 2mm cubes

100g shelled walnuts, finely chopped

120g cooked and peeled chestnuts, crushed into crumbs

8–12 rashers of streaky bacon, rind removed

300ml dry cider

For the coleslaw

1 kohlrabi or celeriac (approx. 150g), peeled and grated

½ an apple, unpeeled, grated

a squeeze of lemon juice

2 tbsp olive oil

Preheat the oven to 200°C. Season the chicken thighs on both sides with salt and pepper. Spread out each thigh, skin side down. Chop half a shallot very finely and mix it with the apple, walnuts and chestnuts. Divide the stuffing between the middle of each thigh then fold over the sides of the meat so it covers the stuffing and joins in the middle. Secure with a cocktail stick through each end and one through the middle.

Wrap 2 or 3 rashers of bacon around the sides, securing them with a cocktail stick at each end. Take a length of butcher's string and wrap up the chicken parcel as though it were a package.

Chop the rest of the shallots roughly and scatter in a baking dish. Arrange the chicken thighs on top and pour in the cider. Cook in the oven for 45 minutes.

Just before serving make the coleslaw by mixing together the kohlrabi and apple. Squeeze over a little lemon juice, drizzle with the oil and season with salt.

Remove the cocktail sticks from the chicken and serve with the salad. Drizzle some of the remaining pan juices over the top.

Une petite astuce – tip Don't make the coleslaw too far in advance, as the apple will turn brown.

Paris-Brest salé

SAVOURY PARIS-BREST

Legend has it that the original Paris-Brest, now a classic among French pastries, was created by chef patissier Louis Durand in 1910 to celebrate the famous Paris-Brest bicycle race. The traditional version is a simple choux pastry ring (or bicycle tyre, as the shape represents) filled with a voluptuous praline cream. In homage to my trip from Paris to Brest I took inspiration from one of my favourite Parisian ingredients to transform this classic pastry into a savoury delight. Instead of praline cream this Paris-Brest is filled with Brie de Meaux, some delicious crunchy apples and a little fresh spinach. A zingy mustard mousse ties everything together.

Makes 6

Preparation time: 30 minutes
Cooking time: 20–25 minutes
Equipment: a piping bag with a 10mm nozzle

1 x choux pastry recipe
(see page 274)

icing sugar, to dust

6 tbsp chopped hazelnuts

For the mustard mousse

50g whipping cream

1 tbsp wholegrain mustard

1 egg white

For the filling

150g Brie de Meaux (or other Brie), mature Comté or Cheddar finely sliced

2 small apples, cored and finely sliced

100g baby spinach leaves

Start by making the choux pastry (see page 274). Scrape the dough into a piping bag fitted with a 10mm nozzle. Line several baking trays with baking paper, dotting a little of the pastry dough in each corner to help the paper stick.

Preheat the oven to 180°C. Use a 10cm plate to draw 6 circles on the baking paper. Pipe a ring of the choux pastry just inside one of the lines. Pipe a second ring tightly inside the first ring, so they are touching. Pipe a third ring on top of the two. Dust with icing sugar and sprinkle 1 tablespoon of the hazelnuts over the top. Repeat with the other circle outlines. Bake in the oven for 20–25 minutes or until well-risen and golden brown.

Whisk the cream until whipped and then stir in the mustard. In a clean grease-free glass or metal bowl whisk the egg whites until they form firm peaks. Fold the egg whites into the cream and pour into a piping bag or a freezer bag with the corner snipped off. (Alternatively you can just use a spoon to dollop the cream on to the filling in the next step.)

When the pastry is cooked it should be golden on the top and base. Remove from the oven and leave to cool for 5 minutes before slicing each ring in half horizontally. Lay slices of cheese on the choux pastry bases, followed by slices of apple. Pipe little dollops of the mustard mousse on top of the apples, or spoon on. Scatter over the spinach and carefully replace the top of the choux pastry ring. Serve immediately.

Faire en avance – get ahead The choux pastry rings can be made a day in advance. Simply place on a baking tray and cook in an oven preheated to 160°C for 10 minutes to crisp up.

Les kouignettes aux groseilles

BUTTERY REDCURRANT PASTRIES

Kouignettes are mini versions of the famous Brittany pastry, *kouign-amann*. It took at least three days of pointing at the cake in patisseries before I got my head around the pronunciation (the literal translation from the Breton dialect is 'butter cake'). The simplest way to think of it is 'queen' plus 'am-an'. Or in the case of my miniature versions, 'queen' plus 'et'.

The traditional cake is not much more than a simple combination of butter and sugar, layered in the same way as puff pastry, but between a yeasted dough. You can tell a good *kouign-amman* just by looking at it (beware of pale imitations masquerading as the real thing); it should have a crunchy, deep caramel-coloured shell, a sign it has been baked long and hot enough to make the pastry crisp and the sugar caramelized.

Just a little note re: technique. This recipe takes some understanding. Read the instructions through a couple of times if you're embarking on this for the first time and also have a look at the photos on page 44.

Makes 12
Preparation time: 1 hour • Resting time: 2 hours, or overnight • Cooking time: 30 minutes
Equipment: a 12-cup muffin tin

260g plain white flour, plus extra for dusting • 1 tsp instant dried yeast • 1 tsp salt • 180ml warm water • 200g butter, frozen for 30 minutes • 1 tbsp soft butter, for greasing • 150g sugar • 2 handfuls of lingonberries (or red- or blackcurrants), frozen or fresh and removed from the stem

Mix together the flour, yeast and salt. Add the water and continue to mix until it forms a ball (if the dough is very dry add a tablespoon more water). Remove from the bowl and knead for at least 10 minutes or until the dough is smooth. Place back in the bowl, cover with cling film and leave in a warm place for 1 hour.

Cut the chilled butter into very thin slices (roughly 2mm thick). Leave in the fridge until needed.

Dust the work surface lightly with flour. Roll out the dough to a rectangle roughly 30cm x 40cm, with the short side facing you. Place the butter slices in the middle of the dough; they can overlap slightly. The butter should cover about half of the dough, leaving a quarter of the dough all the way round like a frame.

Fold the top and bottom edges of dough over the butter to meet in the middle. Take the rolling pin and press down gently all over the dough. Do the same again, folding the top quarter over and the bottom quarter up to meet in the middle.

Fold the top half over the bottom half and turn the pastry round so that you have the seam on the left (like a book). Roll out the dough again to a rectangle about 30cm x 40cm, with the short side facing you. Fold the bottom edge over to the middle, and fold the top down to meet it in the middle. Then fold the top half over the bottom half once more (this process is called a roll and fold). Wrap the dough tightly in cling film (it will expand) and leave it to rest in the fridge for at least 2 hours, or preferably overnight.

Grease the muffin tin with the soft butter and leave in the fridge until needed.

When the dough has rested, put a baking tray in the oven and preheat the oven to 200°C. Sprinkle your work surface liberally with some of the sugar. Place the dough on top of the sugar (with the seam on the left) and sprinkle it with more sugar. Roll out the dough to a large rectangle about 30cm x 40cm, with the long side facing you. Add more sugar to the work surface if the dough begins to stick. Sprinkle the rest of the sugar on top of the pastry and scatter over the berries. Roll up the dough tightly and cut into 12 equal slices. Place each *kouignette* in the muffin tin, put the muffin tin on the preheated baking tray and cook for 25 minutes until the *kouignettes* are a deep golden brown. Remove from the oven and leave to cool for 5 minutes before removing them from the tin. Do not leave to cool completely in the tin, otherwise they will get stuck.

Les petites astuces – tips Cold hands and a cool kitchen will make this dough easier to handle. Run your hands under cold water before handling the pastry. If you have a metal, marble or laminate work surface, place a large tray filled with ice cubes on the work surface for 30 minutes before adding the butter to the dough.

Faire en avance – get ahead You can freeze the *kouignettes* before baking. Defrost before baking.

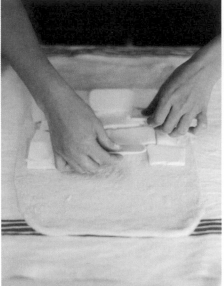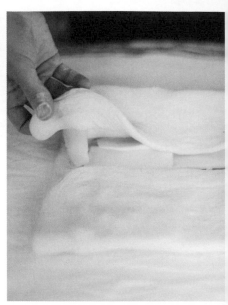

Phares au caramel, gingembre et framboise

CARAMEL, GINGER AND RASPBERRY LIGHTHOUSES

Lighthouses are a quintessential sight along the Breton coast, as the waters around these ways are dangerous to navigate, with jagged rocks cropping up from nowhere. These iconic beacons of light have become a symbol of Brittany and can be spotted not only along the coast, but also in the many souvenir shops alongside the famous stripy tops. When it comes to ornamental souvenirs I'm not that fussed, but edible ones? That's a whole different matter.

Serves 4

Preparation time: 40 minutes

Cooking time: 40 minutes

Resting time: 1 hour

Equipment: a piping bag with an 8mm nozzle

½ x choux pastry recipe (see page 274)

16 raspberries (approx. 50g)

1 x quantity of salted butter caramel (see page 48)

icing sugar, for dusting

For the ginger cream

6 egg yolks

80g sugar

40g cornflour

1–2 tsp ground ginger

500ml full-fat milk

Start by making the choux pastry (see page 274). Scrape the dough into a piping bag fitted with a 8mm nozzle. Line two baking trays with baking paper, dotting a little of the pastry dough in each corner to help the paper stick.

Preheat the oven to 180°C. Hold the nozzle at a 90-degree angle about 5mm from the lined tray. Keep it nozzle upright and pipe 4 small walnut-sized balls of dough, leaving a 3cm gap between each one (they should be about 3cm wide). Then pipe 4 slightly larger balls of dough on the same tray. If any of the balls have little points, dip your finger in some water and gently pat the points down, otherwise they will burn in the oven.

On the second tray, pipe 4 balls of dough that are a little bigger than the previous ones, and then pipe another 4 balls of dough, again, slightly bigger than the last set. These final balls should be about 4cm wide.

Dust with icing sugar before cooking in the preheated oven. After 20 minutes remove the tray with the smaller buns, and 10 minutes later remove the second tray. Leave to cool.

While the buns are cooking, make the pastry cream. Whisk the egg yolks with the sugar until light and thick, then whisk in the cornflour. Add the ginger to the milk in a small saucepan. Bring the milk to the boil and then turn off the heat. Pour the milk in a slow stream over the egg mixture, whisking vigorously all the time.

Pour the mixture into a clean saucepan and continuously whisk over a medium heat. Make sure to scrape the sides and the bottom, otherwise it will burn. The cream will start to thicken and once it releases a bubble or two, remove from the heat.

Line a shallow baking tray with cling film and pour in the creamy mixture. Cover with cling film (so it rests directly on the surface of the cream) and refrigerate for at least an hour. When ready to use, beat with a whisk until smooth and place in a piping bag.

Cut a small slit in the bottom of a choux bun. Hold it between your thumb and index finger with the slit facing up and squeeze gently so it opens. Push in a raspberry then fill with the pastry cream. Repeat with all the buns.

Stack 4 choux buns on top of each other with the largest at the bottom and the smallest at the top. Use some caramel sauce to stick them together. Pierce the bamboo skewers through the middle to keep the lighthouse upright while assembling the others.

Just before serving, remove the skewers. Pour more sauce over the top and add a raspberry to the top. I like to add a flag for the true lighthouse effect.

Caramel au beurre salé

SALTED BUTTER CARAMEL

It was only a matter of time before somebody in Brittany discovered that combining the region's staples of butter and cream with sugar and a pinch of salt, and then cooking it, could make something so utterly moreish. That hit of salt in Breton caramel turns a quite plain caramel into something very special. And the caramel is taken a shade darker than usual to create a slightly bitter note, which balances out the sugary sweetness. I love adding a spoon of this to my morning yoghurt.

Makes approx. 250g
Preparation time: 5 minutes
Cooking time: 15 minutes
Equipment: a kitchen thermometer

150g sugar

100ml double cream

40g golden syrup or runny honey

40g butter

½ tsp salt

Add half the sugar to a clean saucepan with 2 tablespoons of water. Place over a medium to high heat and leave to melt. Do not stir, instead swirl the saucepan around gently.

Once the caramel has turned a dark reddish-brown, remove the pan from the heat and add the rest of the ingredients. Be careful not to stand over the pan as you do so, as the caramel will steam and bubble a lot. Give the pan a good swirl and then return it to a medium heat. Cook for 3–4 minutes or until it reaches 113°C.

Remove from the heat and leave to cool for a couple of minutes before pouring into a glass jar. Scrape all the caramel from the pan using a heat-resistant spatula. It will keep for a couple of months in the fridge; reheat and add a little water to thin it out.

To make soft-set caramels
Continue to cook the caramel over a medium heat until it reaches 127°C. Pour into a small baking dish or a baking tin lined with baking paper. Leave to set before using a knife dipped in boiling water to cut into squares.

Les petites astuces – tips For spiced caramel, add 1 tsp cinnamon and ½ tsp ground ginger; for a zingy touch, add the zest of 1 orange and 1 lemon; for a chocolately finish, stir in 3 tbsp cocoa nibs.

Tartelettes Far Breton

PRUNE AND CUSTARD TARTLETS

Far Bretons are as ubiquitous as *Phares Bretonnes* in Brittany (the same pronunciation, but definitely not to be confused with the lighthouses). The *Far Breton* is a dense flan, similar to Limousin's *clafoutis* but studded with prunes, which takes its name from the Latin word for wheat. It was originally an economical dessert, simply sweetened with dried fruits, such as raisins or prunes. I love a slice of flan but I prefer mine to have a crisp caramelized crust to contrast with the soft squidgy centre like these bite-sized morsels.

Makes 12

Preparation time: 30 minutes
Cooking time: 35 minutes
Equipment: a 12-cup muffin tin

1 tbsp soft butter, for greasing

4 tbsp sugar

350g puff pastry

For the filling

12 soft, ready-to-eat pitted prunes (approx. 100g)

300ml crème fraîche

4 tbsp sugar

2 eggs, plus 1 egg yolk

a pinch of salt

Grease the muffin tin with the butter.

Dust the work surface with some sugar and roll out the pastry to a large rectangle about 40cm x 30cm, with the long side facing you. Dust with sugar and gently roll with a rolling pin to press in the sugar.

Roll up the dough tightly and cut into 12 equal-sized slices. Place each slice, cut side up in the muffin tin. Using your thumb push the dough outwards and upwards to evenly to coat the inside of each cup, until it reaches the top.

Preheat the oven to 190°C. Place a prune in each tartelette. Whisk together the filling ingredients and then fill each tartlet to 3mm from the top. Bake for 35 minutes or until the pastry is golden. Remove immediately from the tin and place on a wire rack to cool.

Les petites astuces – tips The prunes can be replaced with other soft fruit such as apricots, dried soft apples, a few raspberries or cherries – or you can simply leave them out for a plain version.

Make sure to remove the *tartelettes* from the tin immediately, otherwise they will get stuck from the sugar caramelizing.

Faire en avance – get ahead They will keep for two days in an airtight container.

Yaourts aux coulis de framboise

RASPBERRY RIPPLE YOGHURT

After Germany, the French are the biggest consumers of yoghurt in Europe; the vast selection in the supermarket gives that away. And it's not just plain yoghurt or fruit-flavoured varieties, but also yoghurts made from goat's and sheep's milk. Yoghurt isn't something you'd immediately think of making at home, as many people think you need a machine to achieve the right results. Determined to prove this was not the case (there is no more room in my little Paris kitchen for cookbooks, so a yoghurt machine is out of the question), I set about testing out some recipes using my tiny oven. *Et voila!*

Makes 4–6 small pots
Preparation time: 10 minutes
Resting time: 7 hours
Cooking time: 3 hours
Equipment: 4–6 x 175g glass yoghurt pots or ramekins; a kitchen thermometer (optional)

300g frozen raspberries

40g sugar

¼ tsp freshly grated tonka bean or ½ a vanilla pod, split lengthways and seeds scraped out

500ml full-fat organic milk

70g full-fat milk powder

70g organic full-fat plain 'live' yoghurt

2 tbsp crème fraîche

To make the raspberry coulis, place the raspberries, sugar and tonka bean in a small saucepan. Place over a medium heat to defrost, stirring occasionally. Once it has come to the boil, remove from the heat. Use a stick blender to break up the raspberries and pips (pass it through a sieve if you prefer a pip-free version). Divide the raspberry coulis between the yoghurt pots and chill in the fridge until needed.

Place the milk and milk powder in a small saucepan and scald (you want to heat it to just before it starts simmering; 82°C). Remove from the heat and leave to cool until you can comfortably dip your finger in the milk. Whisk in the yoghurt and crème fraîche, making sure the yoghurt completely blends into the milk. Carefully ladle the mixture into the yoghurt pots.

Place the pots in the oven at 50°C and leave for 3 hours without opening the door. Turn off and leave for a further 6 hours. Chill in the fridge for at least an hour before eating.

Une petite astuce – tip Use an oven thermometer to accurately test the temperature of the oven. If the oven is too hot, the bacteria will be killed off.

Faire en avance – get ahead The yoghurt will keep in the fridge for up to a week.

Galette des rois

KING'S CAKE

This has to be one of my favourite French traditions. January in England is barren of gastronomic fun, with everyone spending the post-Christmas period on some form of diet. In France, on the other hand, this is the time to celebrate Epiphany on the 6 January with a rich frangipane *galette*. Captured in the *galette* is what they call the *fève*, which was originally a dried fava bean. These days a fancier little porcelain figurine is used, and whoever is lucky enough to land on the slice which contains it – without breaking a tooth – gets the honour of wearing a gold paper crown. Normally the *galette* is more like a pie, with the puff pastry completely encasing the almond cream, but I prefer to cover mine with a layer of apples for a bit of a sharp contrast.

Serves 6–8

Preparation time: 30 minutes

Resting time: 30 minutes

Cooking time: 45 minutes

Equipment: an 18cm springform cake tin, depth 7cm; 1 tiny ceramic figurine or a clean penny; 1 gold paper crown

100g very soft butter, plus a little extra for greasing

350g puff pastry

150g shelled blanched hazelnuts

75g sugar

a pinch of salt

1 egg

1 apple, unpeeled, cored and finely sliced

Line the bottom of the cake tin with baking paper and butter the sides. Cut the puff pastry in half and roll out one half to fit the base of the cake tin, trimming away any excess. Roll out the other half to a rectangle 15cm x 35cm and cut it in half lengthways.

Line the sides of the cake tin with one of the pastry strips allowing a little overlap where the base meets the side. Use your fingertip to press down the overlap to make sure the pastry seals. Push the second half around the bottom of the tin, where the sides and base join, allowing a little overlap.

Using a sharp knife cut out triangles from the side to create a crown shape. Make sure to leave a band at least 3.5cm high around the base otherwise the hazelnut cream will spill out. Chill the lined tin in the fridge for 30 minutes.

Toast the hazelnuts in a dry pan until golden. Leave to cool slightly before blending to a fine powder. Beat together the sugar, hazelnuts, salt and butter until smooth, then incorporate the egg. Spread the mixture evenly over the base of the pastry. Hide the small ceramic figure or the penny in the pastry cream and cover with the sliced apple.

Place a baking tray in the oven and preheat it to 200°C. Put the cake in the oven on the hot tray and reduce the temperature to 180°C. Bake for 45 minutes or until golden brown. If the pastry browns too quickly cover with some greased foil.

Bordeaux

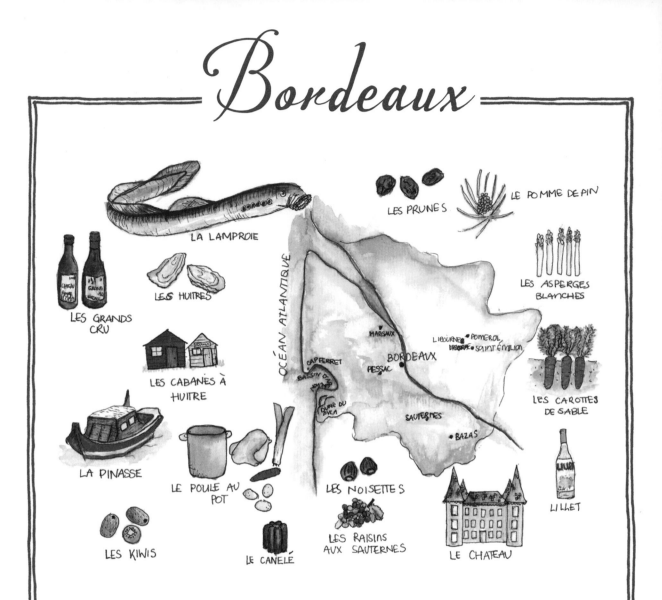

LA LAMPROIE

LES PRUNES

LE POMME DE PIN

LES GRANDS CRU

LES HUITRES

OCÉAN ATLANTIQUE

LES ASPERGES BLANCHES

LES CABANES À HUITRE

MARGAUX

LIBOURNE · POMEROL
LIBOURNE · SAINT ÉMILION

BORDEAUX

CAP FERRET

BASSIN D'ARCACHON

PESSAC

DUNE DU PYLA

SAUTERNES

BAZAS

LES CAROTTES DE SABLE

LA PINASSE

LE POULE AU POT

LES NOISETTES

LILLET

LES KIWIS

LE CANELÉ

LES RAISINS AUX SAUTERNES

LE CHATEAU

ELEGANT CHATEAUX, CHICKEN IN POTS AND RICKETY OYSTER SHACKS

The majestic city of Bordeaux sits on *La Garonne*, a riverfront once lined with factories pumping out pollution. For many years, Bordeaux's bourgeois limestone buildings were coated with a thick layer of soot, developed over decades, even centuries, from the dirty emissions expelled by Bordeaux's big industries. In the mid-nineties, *La Belle Endormie*, 'the sleeping beauty' (Bordeaux's nickname), was awoken from its deep sleep with a rejuvenating program which saw the buildings scrubbed clean, the disused warehouses and factories along the river refurbished into smart new offices and apartments and where a shiny new tram now glides effortlessly through the streets.

When I arrived in Bordeaux, there was little evidence of these historically black facades; quite the contrary, as everything was gleaming white. Having a nosy along the cobbled streets of this vibrant town, it felt rather like a mini Paris with its grand symmetrical houses, fountains and polished sculptures. *La Port de la Lune*, once an industrial active harbour, is now home to chic cafés, joggers and open-air food markets at the weekend. Prosperity, mainly generated by Bordeaux's most famous export, wine, is everywhere to behold and proudly so.

Being a trained pastry chef, I had something more on my agenda than simply glugging a good glass of Chateau Margaux. *Cannelé*, caramelized little cakes with a gooey custardy centre, are a local specialty. In search of perfection, I tried endless pastry shops, even a dedicated *cannelé* shop, but none compared to Alain Guignard's creations at his *patisserie* in Arcachon, a pretty seaside town southwest of Bordeaux; I had to recreate them in my own kitchen (page 98).

Cap Ferret is the southwest's answer to St Tropez, though rather more laidback, nestled in the Arcachon Bay. Walking along the beach on a clear day you can see all around the bay, spotting small fishing boats bopping about, big poles jutting out of the water with oyster cages tied to them and plenty of colourful little fisherman's shacks and wooden beach houses lining the coast. This is prime oyster territory, and often the oysters don't make it further than Bordeaux, as they're so prized by the locals.

Gazing out across the bay on a clear day, you'll see a wide expanse of golden sand, the Dune of Pyla. From a distance its size is deceptive, but this sand dune is actually the tallest in Europe, and quite a trek to the top (see page 95). It certainly felt like being in a desert, the sand seemingly extending for miles, like the Sahara of France.

Heading back inland you will undoubtedly discover a dozen chateaux, if not more, with rows and rows of vines. Bordeaux is one of France's most productive wine regions, home to the most expensive reds in the world. However, the area wasn't known internationally for its wines until Henry Platagenet, who eventually became King Henry II of England, married Eleanor of Aquitaine in the twelfth century, making the Aquitaine territory English. He exported a large amount of Bordeaux claret in exchange for other goods, and spread the wine and its reputation throughout the world. As well as the great reds of Margaux, Saint-Emilion and Pomerol, the sweet Sauternes holds a lot of clout too. You'll spot delis selling prunes, raisins and other dried fruit that have been soaked in this perfumed sweet wine, sometimes then covered in chocolate, making for delightful little nibbles.

I started to feel that there was a bit of a class system going on with the region's gastronomy. Wine was labelled *Premier Cru*, *Grand Cru Classé* or *Vin de Table*, oysters were graded 0–5, with the smaller the number signifying the bigger oyster, and asparagus was sold by its thickness. But, while the gastronomy seemed a little elitist, the cobbled streets of Bordeaux certainly didn't. There was a vibrant mix of food from all over the world alongside a handful of classic French eateries. Bordeaux has a big university and, after speaking to a young Bordelais chef and restaurant owner, Aurélien Crosato, I learned that the majority of students are looking for a meal that fills you up without emptying your wallet, rather than a gourmet experience.

The wine flows generously in Bordeaux, at mealtimes and in the kitchen preparations. Whether you're trying out my quick red wine roast chicken (on page 76) or the sweet seasoning of Sauternes in my crispy duck wraps (page 80), wine proves to be a handy and delicious kitchen condiment. I can also recommend a glass of Saint-Emilion to enjoy whilst cooking, because it hits the spot perfectly when winding down after a long day. Just leave the knife skills to someone else.

Huîtres avec un bouillon Bordelais

OYSTERS IN A BORDELAIS BOUILLON

Little oyster shacks dot the Arcachon bay, which is just under an hour's drive west of Bordeaux. Along the coastal route are the so-called *villages ostréicoles*, which, in a nutshell, are like mini Disney Worlds for oyster lovers. One particularly picturesque example is that of the Village de L'Herbe, where rickety seafood shacks with decking spill on to the beach and serve a dozen oysters with a glass of Tariquet for just a few euros.

Traditionally, oysters are simply shucked and served with a squeeze of lemon, but I'm combining them with another typical taste of the region: a hefty Bordeaux red from the nearby Médoc. A deep, rich bouillon is made using the red wine, which is then poured over the oysters to cook them quickly and give them a more meaty texture.

Makes 12 oysters
Preparation time: 15 minutes
Cooking time: 30 minutes

a large knob of butter

2 shallots, peeled and finely sliced

150ml red Bordeaux wine (or another hearty red wine)

500ml hot beef stock

a pinch of salt

2 tbsp red wine vinegar

12 oysters

coarse sea salt

1 tbsp finely chopped chives

Melt the butter in a non-stick saucepan and fry the shallots until golden and caramelized. Add the wine, bring to the boil and then boil for 10 minutes. Add the hot beef stock and salt, and boil vigorously for 5 minutes. Turn off the heat and stir in the vinegar. Taste for seasoning and add a little extra salt if needed.

While the bouillon is boiling, open the oysters. Use a special oyster knife (called a shucker) that has a guard and a dull blade with a pointed tip. Don't even attempt to use an ordinary knife.

Wash and scrub the oysters under cold running water. Using a folded tea towel to protect your hand, place the oyster with its round bottom on a chopping board. Dig the tip of the shucker into the hinge (the pointy end of the oyster) and wiggle the blade along the hinge in order to loosen it then twist the knife to open the shell a little. Keep the knife flush with the top shell and slide it along to separate the two shells and sever the muscle in the top half. Lift off the top shell and remove any broken pieces from the oyster flesh. Should the oyster smell in any way fishy or 'off', discard it. Freshly shucked oysters should smell of the sea in a clean, fresh and pleasant way.

Carefully detach the muscle from the bottom shell with the tip of the knife and drain away any remaining juices from the oyster. Sit the oysters on a bed of sea salt so they are stable. Ladle over the boiling bouillon and sprinkle with the chives. Serve immediately.

Tartare de crabe et kiwi

CRAB AND KIWI TARTARE

I always think of the kiwi as an exotic fruit with its fuzzy brown outside concealing a bright green, juicy centre. But, as I travelled around the region, they kept popping up at food markets and in fruit bowls at breakfast and I was pleasantly surprised to find out that they have been grown in the Landes region, just south of Bordeaux, since the 1960s. Not only does their vibrant colour and zing bring a welcome freshness to the bleak winter fruit selection (the harvest takes place in October and November, making January the best month for eating them), but also their sweet acidity marries beautifully with the local seafood. Chopped up and tossed with some sweet crabmeat and crunchy cucumber, you'll have a fine little starter.

Serves 4 as a starter
Preparation time: 20 minutes

½ a lime

80g chilled crabmeat (brown and white meat)

2 ripe kiwis, peeled and cut into small cubes

1 shallot, peeled and finely chopped

10cm piece of cucumber, deseeded and cut into small cubes

salt

4 slices of bread

1 tbsp unsalted soft butter

Add half a teaspoon of lime zest to a bowl then flake in the crabmeat. Add the kiwi, shallot and cucumber then squeeze over the juice from the lime and toss to coat the ingredients. Taste and season with salt.

Toast the bread and cut into triangles. Spread with the butter and arrange on a plate next to a bowl of the crab tartare.

Une petite astuce – tip For an especially pretty starter, use an 8cm biscuit cutter to cut out 4 circles from the toast. Spread with the butter then place the biscuit cutter on top and fill with the crab tartare to create neat mounds.

Arcachon Bay

POINTES - - - - - - 9
COURTES - - - - - - 8.50
LONGUES - - - - - - 8
12.16 - - - - - - 7.50
                    7.
TÊTES VERTES - - - - 5
FINES bolais - - - -

ASPERGES

Beyond the chateaux and vineyards of Bordeaux in March/April time you might spot covered fields. Hiding under the dustbin-liner black sheets are asparagus, buried deep in the ground. Timing is of fundamental importance when harvesting, as a day or two late and the asparagus will have purple-green tips and can no longer be sold as prized white asparagus.

Asperges blanches habillées

WHITE ASPARAGUS IN BLANKETS

When I visit producers I always like to find out how they like to eat what they produce. Usually it's the simplest way of cooking: a quick blanch, a lick of flame on the barbecue or a speedy steam. While visiting the Perroto family's asparagus farm, Monsieur preferred his white asparagus blanched and served with a knob of butter and a sprinkle of salt, whereas Madame whisked up a quick asparagus omelette with a splash of white wine and served it with some Bayonne ham. When I was there, I tasted white spears fresh out of the ground. They were so sweet, delicate and crunchy that they barely warranted any culinary attention whatsoever, but rarely will food miles be so minute.

Makes 8

Preparation time: 30 minutes
Cooking time: 20 minutes

8 white asparagus spears

salt

3 eggs

100ml milk

a small bunch of chives, finely chopped (approx. 15g)

8 slices of Bayonne or Parma ham

Trim off the tough ends from the asparagus spears and peel the lower part about 5cm up the stem. Bring a large saucepan of salted water to the boil. Add the asparagus to the boiling water and blanch for 4–5 minutes, until they are just tender (test with a sharp knife). Plunge into a bowl of iced water to stop them cooking.

Heat a large non-stick frying pan over a medium to high heat. In a bowl whisk together the eggs, milk, chives and a pinch of salt. When the pan is hot, remove it from the heat, pour in a small ladleful of the egg mixture and quickly swirl it around the pan to make a large pancake. Return the pan to the heat and cook for a couple of minutes. Using a palette knife, gently peel back the pancake and turn it over. Cook for another couple of minutes or until lightly golden. Repeat with the rest of the batter. Keep the pancakes on a plate and cover with foil while you make the rest.

Cut each pancake in half and wrap one half and a slice of Bayonne ham around each asparagus stem.

Les petites astuces – tips You can replace the chives with any other aromatic herbs you might have, such as dill, parsley or marjoram.

If you want to keep this vegetarian, add a handful of finely grated mature cheese to the egg mixture and omit the ham.

Faire en avance – get ahead The asparagus can be cooked a day in advance, kept in the fridge and eaten cold.

Baguette aux goujons et purée de petits pois

FISHFINGER AND MUSHY PEA BAGUETTE

Bordeaux and Britain share a love affair that started back in the twelfth century, when Duchess Eleanor of Aquitaine married Count Henri Platagenet, who then became King Henry II of England. The wine trade flourished during this period and England remained a big importer of claret up until the Battle of Castillon in 1453, when France annexed Britain. I wanted to pay tribute to this Franco-Anglo connection, and what better way than with the marriage of baguette with one of my guilty pleasures: fishfingers.

Serves 4 as a snack

Preparation time: 15 minutes
Cooking time: 15–20 minutes

250g firm white fish (pollock, cod or monkfish), skinned and deboned

4 tbsp plain white flour

salt and freshly ground pepper

2 egg whites, lightly beaten

50g fresh white breadcrumbs

2 tbsp sunflower or vegetable oil

1 baguette

½ a lemon

4 generous tbsp crème fraîche

For the pea purée

1 shallot, peeled and finely sliced

1 clove of garlic, peeled and minced

a generous knob of butter

250g frozen peas

50ml hot chicken or vegetable stock

1 tsp lemon juice

1 tsp lemon zest

a pinch of sugar

To make the purée, gently fry the shallot and garlic in the butter until soft and translucent. Throw in the peas and cook until the peas are soft. Add the hot stock and remove from the heat. Blend to a smooth paste in a food processor. Season, to taste, with salt and add the lemon juice, zest and sugar.

Cut the fish into finger-sized pieces and pat dry with kitchen towel. Lay out three plates or shallow bowls in front of you. Tip the flour into one and season with a pinch of salt and pepper. Pour the egg whites into another and spread out the breadcrumbs on the third. Dip the fish pieces in the flour and dust off any excess. Dip each piece in the egg whites and then roll in the breadcrumbs, making sure the fish is well coated.

Heat the oil in a large frying pan. Once hot, add the goujons (you may have to fry them in batches – don't overcrowd the pan) and cook for about 3 minutes in total, turning halfway, until they are a deep golden brown. Place on a wire rack.

Cut the baguette in half lengthways. Zest half a teaspoon of zest from the lemon and then cut the lemon into 4 pieces. Mix the lemon zest with the crème fraîche and spread it along one side of the baguette. Spread the pea purée along the other side and place the goujons in the middle. Cut into quarters and serve with the lemon wedges on the side.

Tourin à la tomate froide et perles du Japon

CHILLED ROASTED TOMATO SOUP WITH TAPIOCA

If you feel a cold coming on then a classic *tourin à l'ail* is very much called for. Quite simply a garlic soup with tapioca or vermicelli noodles, some variations call for as many as twenty cloves of garlic, while others opt for onions. When tomatoes are in their prime season, this version makes their sweet acidity sing, capturing sunshine in a bowl. I've turned the traditional dish on its head with my chilled version, which uses the juice of fresh tomatoes and the intense sweetness of slow-roasted ones. Throw in some Japanese pearls (the French term sounds so much better than tapioca) and you'll have a delicious dish that celebrates the season.

Serves 4
Preparation time: 30 minutes
Cooking time: 1 hour

750g large ripe tomatoes

500g tomatoes, assorted sizes and colours

3–4 tbsp olive oil

1 clove of garlic, peeled and crushed

sea salt

100g tapioca or vermicelli noodles

1 spring onion, finely chopped

Blend the large tomatoes in a food processor until smooth. Line a sieve with 2 layers of muslin or a clean tea towel and place the sieve over a large bowl. Pour half the tomato purée into the lined sieve. Twist over the ends of the fabric and squeeze out all the juice. Scrape out and discard the pulp and repeat with the rest of the tomato purée. Set the tomato water to one side.

Preheat the oven to 120°C. Halve any cherry tomatoes and quarter the larger ones. Place in a bowl and toss in a couple of tablespoons of the oil and the garlic, and sprinkle with salt. Arrange the tomato pieces on a baking tray and cook in the oven for 1 hour.

Meanwhile cook the tapioca in boiling water according to the packet instructions.

When you're ready to eat, divide the tomato water, tapioca and the roasted tomatoes between serving bowls. Sprinkle the spring onion over the top and drizzle with the rest of the oil.

Une petite astuce – tip Try not to blend the tomatoes for too long as this will result in lots of froth, which will make the juice cloudy. If you do get froth on the top of the juice, simply pass it back through a sieve.

Faire en avance – get ahead The tomato water can be made a couple of days in advance and kept in the fridge.

Poule-au-pot avec riz d'ail croustillant

CHICKEN IN A POT WITH CRISPY GARLIC RICE

A chicken cooking in a pot is still the very essence of home cooking in the Bordeaux region, and how I first experienced it when I stayed at Chateau Lestange. The log fire was raging, the hen was cooking in a pot on the stove, and the estate's rosé wine was flowing. The *poule-au-pot* arrived at the table surgically dissected and arranged on a tray. Mustard and a dish of artfully arranged carrots, potatoes and leeks followed, and we doused everything in white sauce. My version is a little more streamlined – I've replaced the sauce with a punchy cornichon and mustard relish. Crispy garlic rice adds a fantastic texture.

Serves 4
Preparation time: 30 minutes • Cooking time: 2 hours

1 whole chicken (approx. 1.5kg) • 2 onions, peeled and quartered • 4 carrots, peeled and halved lengthways • 10 black peppercorns • 5 juniper berries • 4 bay leaves • 300g lean sausage meat • 75g chicken livers, rinsed, patted dry and very finely minced • 1 clove of garlic, peeled and finely minced • ½ tsp freshly ground pepper • 1 tsp orange zest • *For the rice:* 300g basmati rice • a generous knob of butter • 2 cloves of garlic, peeled and finely minced • a pinch of salt • *For the relish:* 2 heaped tbsp capers, drained and finely chopped • 12 cornichons, drained and finely chopped • a handful of fresh flat-leaf parsley, finely chopped • 2 heaped tsp grainy mustard

Put the chicken, onions, carrots, peppercorns, juniper berries and bay leaves in a large pot. Pour in cold water to just cover the chicken then put the lid on and simmer over a gentle heat for 2 hours.

Mix together the sausage meat, livers, garlic, pepper and orange zest. Mould into a fat sausage shape on a large piece of foil. Roll up tightly and twist the ends to seal the foil like a Christmas cracker. Prick it foil all over with a fork so the flavours can infuse the broth, then nestle it in the pot with the chicken (making sure it's submerged in the stock) for the last 30 minutes of the chicken's cooking time.

Put the rice in a small saucepan and ladle over 600ml of the hot stock from the chicken pot. Cover and boil over a high heat for 7 minutes then drain the rice through a sieve.

In your largest non-stick frying pan (with a lid), melt the butter over a low to medium heat and add the garlic. Gently fry the garlic until it begins to sizzle, then stir in the rice and salt. Wrap the lid of the pan in a clean tea towel and place on top (the tea towel will absorb moisture so the rice stays crispy). Cook for 25 minutes on a very low heat – you want the rice to crisp up on the base of the pan.

Mix together all the relish ingredients. Remove the chicken from the pot and cut into serving-sized pieces. Unwrap the 'stuffing' and slice into rounds. Serve each guest some crispy rice with the chicken, stuffing and carrots. Ladle a little of the hot stock over the top and top with a little relish.

Monsieur Petit, free-range chicken farmer, Avensan

Poulet rôti au vin rouge

ROAST RED WINE CHICKEN

Even in Bordeaux, arguably the wine capital of the world, sometimes you can't quite finish a whole bottle. That's when this marinade comes in handy. A loitering leftover glass of red wine can make for the perfect marinade. If leftover wine is a rare occurrence in your household, donate a little glass from your bottle of red and enjoy a spectacular dish to accompany the remainder of the bottle.

Serves 4–6

Preparation time: 30 minutes

Marinating time: 30 minutes, or overnight

Cooking time: 1 hour

150ml red wine

100g tomato paste

3 sprigs of fresh thyme, leaves picked

3 sprigs of fresh marjoram, leaves picked, or ½ teaspoon dried

100ml red wine vinegar

1 whole chicken cut into 8 pieces (approx. 1.5kg)

salt and freshly ground pepper

500g baby potatoes, washed

3 onions, peeled and quartered

6 carrots, peeled and quartered lengthways

125ml water

Mix together the wine, tomato paste, herbs and vinegar. Season the chicken pieces with plenty of salt and pepper then place in a sealed bag with the marinade. Shake the bag to make sure each piece is well coated. Place in the fridge for at least 30 minutes or overnight.

In the meantime, place the potatoes in a saucepan of cold water, put the lid on top and bring up to the boil. Boil for 1–2 minutes, then drain in a colander.

Arrange the onions, carrots and cooked potatoes in a large baking dish or tray (big enough to fit the chicken and the vegetables) and pour over the water. Preheat the oven to 200°C.

Remove the chicken from the fridge and arrange the pieces, skin side up, in a layer on top of the vegetables in the dish. Pour the rest of the marinade over the chicken. Cover with a sheet of baking paper or foil and roast for 30 minutes. Remove the baking paper or foil and baste the chicken with the cooking liquid. Roast, uncovered, for another 15 minutes or until the skin is crisp. Serve immediately.

Les petites astuces – tips Buying a whole chicken will always work out as being more affordable. If you aren't up for dissecting it yourself, ask your butcher to cut it into pieces for you. If there's no knife-wielding butcher about, you can always cheat and go for chicken thighs.

If you're unsure whether the chicken is cooked through, pierce the flesh with a sharp knife; the juices from the chicken should come out clear.

Faire en avance – get ahead The veg and chicken can be prepared up to a day in advance, then simply pop it all in the baking dish and cook as above.

Le Bouchon Bordelais, Bordeaux

Rouleaux aux canard croustillant et raisins aux Sauternes rôtis

CRISPY DUCK AND ROASTED SAUTERNES GRAPE WRAPS

Duck in France, particularly in the southwest where there are plenty of duck farmers, usually comes in the form of a *confit* (where the duck is cooked and preserved in its own fat) or pâté. Although delicious, making your own can be quite time consuming so I prefer to do away with the hassle of storing the duck in fat by simply roasting it with a few local ingredients, such as grapes and Sauternes, a rather unique sweet wine made in Graves, Bordeaux.

It just so happened that I was testing this recipe in my Paris kitchen on Chinese New Year. Living in Belleville, Paris's second Chinatown, I started thinking about the Chinese love of crispy duck. The roasted grapes in this dish are blended to make a sweet sauce (similar to the sweet plum sauce eaten with Peking duck). Wrap it all in a lettuce leaf with some crunchy cucumber and crisp fresh leeks, and you've got Asian-style French duck!

Serves 4
Preparation time: 20 minutes
Cooking time: 2 hours

2 duck legs

salt

1 tbsp white pepper

250g seedless red grapes or prunes

100ml Sauternes wine, or other sweet white wine

½ a cucumber or 1 small cucumber, washed, halved lengthways and seeds removed

1 small leek

2 tbsp olive oil

juice of ½ a lemon

a pinch of sugar

1 tsp hot chilli sauce

1 romaine or iceberg lettuce, washed and leaves separated

Preheat the oven to 160°C. Season the duck legs liberally with salt and pepper and rub into the skin. Place the duck legs in a baking dish with the grapes and wine. Cover with foil and bake in the preheated oven for 1½ hours. Increase the heat to 200°C then remove the foil and cook for a further 30 minutes (if the skin starts to brown too quickly, turn down the heat or remove from the oven).

While the duck is cooking prepare the salad. Cut the cucumber into 1cm cubes and slice the leek into thin rings. Soak the leek in a bowl of water for 5 minutes to remove any grit. Drain and dry with kitchen towel before placing in a bowl with the cucumber. Toss with the oil, lemon juice and sugar and season with salt.

Once the duck is cooked, remove from the tray and wrap in foil while you prepare the sauce. Put all the grapes and a couple of tablespoons of the cooking liquid in a blender and blitz to a smooth paste. Add chilli sauce and salt, to taste.

Peel the skin off the duck and chop it up. Shred or cut the meat from the bone. Serve the skin and meat with the salad, sauce and lettuce leaves and let everyone help themselves.

Crumble aux fruits de mer

OAT-CRUSTED SEAFOOD CRUMBLE

A savoury crumble, I hear you ask? I questioned it too when I first spotted it on a restaurant menu in Paris. Who would have thought the French would steal a traditional British pudding recipe and make it its own? Bordeaux has a long history with the English, having been under British rule for three hundred years from the middle of the twelfth century. Drawing on this history I wanted to combine some of Bordeaux's wonderful seafood with a classic British cooking technique. As tasty and comforting as a fish pie, but without the hassle of making a creamy sauce or mashed potato topping, that Parisian restaurant was on to a good thing.

Serves 4

Preparation time: 15 minutes
Cooking time: 30 minutes

150g raw tiger prawns, peeled

150g fillet of white fish (cod, monkfish, haddock all work well), skinned and cut into 2.5–3cm pieces

125g leeks, washed, trimmed and cut into 1.5cm pieces

125g cauliflower, broken into 1.5cm florets

350g fromage blanc

1 tsp ground white pepper

1 tsp finely grated lemon zest

a pinch of salt

For the crumble topping

50g cold butter, cut into small cubes

75g wholemeal flour

40g rolled oats

40g pine nuts, roughly chopped

40g mature Comté, Cheddar or other strongly flavoured hard cheese, finely grated

Preheat the oven to 180°C. Mix together all the filling ingredients in a bowl, then divide the mixture between individual ramekins or tip into one large baking dish (approx. 20cm x 26cm).

To make the crumble topping, use your fingertips to rub the butter into the flour until you have a sandy texture, then mix in the oats, pine nuts and cheese. Top the filling with an even layer of the crumble. Bake for 30 minutes, until the top is golden brown.

Une petite astuce – tip Make sure that the cauliflower florets are the same size as the leek pieces; otherwise they won't cook through.

Faire en avance – get ahead The pie can be assembled a day in advance and kept in the fridge until needed.

Brochettes de boeuf avec petits pains plats

BEEF KOFTAS WITH HERBY FLATBREADS

In the week before Shrove Tuesday, in a little town called Bazas, south-east of Bordeaux, you might stumble across a rather bizarre bovine occasion, when cows bearing flowers and ribbons on their head are paraded down the main street. But these aren't just any old cows; they are the prized cult local breed Bazadais, known for the rich marbled fat running through the meat. The beef parade, which has been celebrated annually since 1283, culminates in a brilliant banquet with the Bazadais beef as the centrepiece. Inspired by this shared feast, my dish is a help-yourself affair; perfect for a get-together with friends.

Serves 4

Preparation time: 40 minutes • Cooking time: 30 minutes • Resting time: 1 hour
Equipment: 8 skewers (soaked in cold water if using wooden ones)

1 x herby flatbread recipe (see page 275) • 2 tbsp vegetable oil, for frying • 1 head of romaine lettuce, washed, dried and finely chopped, to serve • *For the koftas:* 300g lean beef mince • 75g veal liver, finely minced or chopped • 1 clove of garlic, peeled and minced • 1 tsp lemon zest, finely grated • a generous pinch of salt • 1 tsp Espelette pepper or mild chilli flakes • 2 tbsp fresh breadcrumbs • a small handful of finely chopped flat-leaf parsley • 1 shallot, peeled and finely chopped • *For the yoghurt sauce:* 250g plain yoghurt • 1 tbsp lemon juice • a pinch of salt • a pinch of sugar

First make the flatbreads (see page 275). After one hour, dust a work surface with a little flour. Divide the dough into 8 pieces and roll out each one into a round about 5mm thick.

Place a non-stick frying pan over a very high heat. Cook the flatbreads one at a time (unless you can comfortably fit two in your pan). Dry-fry for 1–2 minutes, or until bubbles appear and the dough starts to colour, then flip over and cook for another 1–2 minutes on the other side. Keep warm in a tea towel while you cook the others.

To make the yoghurt sauce, mix all the ingredients together. Set aside until needed.

In a bowl, mix all the ingredients for the koftas. Divide into 8 and squeeze on to the skewers. Heat the oil in a large frying pan over a medium to high heat and fry the skewers for 3–4 minutes, turning occasionally until evenly cooked though.

To serve, cut open a flatbread, fill with a kofta and some crunchy lettuce, and drizzle with the yoghurt sauce.

Croustade de pomme et boudin noir

CRUNCHY APPLE AND BLACK PUDDING PIE

The *croustade* (also known as *tourtière*) is a popular Bordeaux treat, comprising layers of thin pastry sandwiching apples or prunes and doused with a sugary Armagnac syrup. What is most fascinating is to see how they make the pastry; a little ball of dough is stretched into a paper-thin pastry sheet the size of a table (have a look online for a video if you can't get to see a Bordeaux boulanger in action). My version gets a savoury addition in the form of some salty and creamy *boudin noir*, which marries beautifully with the tartness of apple.

Serves 4–6 as a starter

Preparation time: 45 minutes
Resting time: 1 hour
Baking time: 30 minutes
Equipment: a 23cm round deep-sided sandwich tin

For the pastry dough

250g plain white flour, plus extra to dust

a pinch of salt

2 tbsp vegetable or other flavourless oil

120ml warm water

sugar

For the filling

75g butter, melted

4 tbsp sugar

1 apple (approx. 150g), cored and cut into 0.5cm slices

200g *boudin noir* or black pudding, skin removed

Mix the flour and salt together in a bowl, then pour in the oil and water. Using your hands, bring the mixture together until it forms a ball (add a drop of water if it seems too dry). Knead until it is smooth (alternatively use the dough hook on a food processor for 5 minutes). Wrap in cling film and leave to rest at room temperature for at least an hour.

Preheat the oven to 200°C. Place a clean fabric tablecloth on a large table and dust with flour. With your knuckles under the dough (palms down), gently start to stretch it out in a circular motion. When it's too big to hold, lay it down in the middle of the floured tablecloth. Use the same method to stretch it out, until the pastry is roughly 60cm x 90cm and paper-thin all over (you should be able to read a newspaper through it!). Trim the edges with scissors. Use a brush to splatter some melted butter on top.

Halve the pastry. Splatter one half with more butter and sprinkle with some sugar. Fold in half, short edges together, and brush off any excess flour on the underside. Repeat with other half.

Place one piece of the pastry in the centre of the tin, leaving the excess hanging over the edge. Splatter with more butter and sprinkle with more sugar. Arrange the apples over the pastry base and crumble the boudin noir on top. Place the second piece of pastry on top and tuck the excess pastry around and underneath the filling to encase it. Brush with butter and dust with sugar.

Fold the overhanging pastry from the base over the top, draping it into the centre. Add another coat of butter and dusting of sugar before cooking in the oven for 30 minutes or until the top and bottom of the pie are golden brown.

Gateau aux carottes et noix de coco

CARROT AND COCONUT CAKE

Carrot cake can hardly be considered an authentic French cake, but with the rise of Anglo-American coffee shops around France, *le gateau aux carottes* is rapidly become a regular fixture alongside scones and crumbles.

Serves 12

Preparation time: 30 minutes

Cooling time: 15 minutes

Baking time: 1–1½ hours

Equipment: an 18cm straight-sided sandwich tin, greased with butter and base-lined

160g soft butter, plus a little extra for greasing

200g golden Demerara sugar

2 tsp ground cinnamon

1 tsp ground ginger

½ tsp ground cardamom

finely grated zest of 1 orange

1 tsp salt

4 eggs

120g plain yoghurt

400g carrots, peeled and roughly grated

400g wholemeal flour

4 tsp baking powder

For the icing

250g crème fraîche

2 tbsp icing sugar

100g desiccated coconut or coconut shavings

Preheat the oven to 180°C. Beat together the butter, sugar, spices, orange zest and salt until fluffy. Beat in the eggs, one at a time, and then mix in the yoghurt and grated carrots. In a separate bowl mix together the flour and baking powder.

Fold the dry ingredients into the wet, then scrape the batter into the prepared tin. Smooth the top to create a roughly even surface. Bake for 1–1½ hours in the preheated oven, until a skewer, when inserted, comes out clean. Leave to cool in its tin before turning out on to a wire rack to cool completely. While the cake cools you can make the icing.

Mix together the crème fraîche and icing sugar until smooth. When the cake is cool, use a spatula to spread the icing over the top and side of the cake, then sprinkle with the coconut.

Les petites astuces – tips The wholemeal flour can be replaced with spelt flour for a lighter cake.

If you're in a rush (or prefer a lighter cake), do away with the icing and simply dust the cake with a little icing sugar before serving.

Faire en avance – get ahead After cooling and before icing, the cake can be wrapped tightly in cling film and frozen for several months. Alternatively, the cake is remarkably moist and will keep, un-iced, for up to three days.

Tarte tatin aux carottes

CARROT TARTE TATIN

Apples are the traditional choice of topping for a tarte tatin but carrots make a delicious savoury alternative. Carrots are a staple in every French household but they are not all the same. In the Landes region of southwest France, a particular type is grown that thrives in sand rather than soil. This technique makes for a flavoursome and juicy carrot, perfect for a simple dish such as this one where the carrot is the star.

Serves 4–6 as a starter
Preparation time: 15 minutes
Cooking time: 45–50 minutes
Equipment: an 18cm round tart tin

8–10 medium carrots (or 5 large, halved lengthways)

2 knobs of butter

3 sprigs of fresh thyme

a good pinch of salt

½ tbsp runny honey

1 tbsp red wine vinegar

250g puff pastry

Preheat the oven to 180°C. Peel the carrots if they have a thick skin, otherwise just wash them well and pat dry.

Melt the butter in a large frying pan over a low heat. When the butter begins to sizzle, add the carrots and thyme. Cook for about 15 minutes, turning the carrots so they brown all over. Remove from the heat, sprinkle with salt and stir in the honey and vinegar so that the carrots are well coated. Arrange them in the bottom of the tart tin.

Roll out the pastry between two sheets of baking paper until it is 5mm thick and cut out a disc that is a just a little bigger than the tart tin. Place on top of the carrots and tuck in the edges. Cut a small cross in the middle (to let the steam from the carrots escape during cooking).

Bake in the preheated oven for 30–35 minutes, or until the pastry is puffy and golden. Place a large serving plate on top of the tin and carefully flip the tarte tatin on to the plate. Serve while still warm with a green salad.

Les petites astuces – tips If you have a tarte tatin tin or an ovenproof frying pan, you can cook the carrots in that and then tuck the pastry directly over the top.

In Paris, ready-made puff pastry is found in a section of the supermarket called 'aide culinaire' (culinary help). And ready-made puff pastry is exactly that: it's there to help you out! Just make sure to buy all-butter puff pastry (the ingredients on the back should only list flour, butter and salt, and maybe a tiny bit of water).

Pruneaux au Cognac et épices

PRUNES IN COGNAC AND SPICES

The town of Agen, about an hour and a half drive southeast of Bordeaux, is famous for its prunes. Now I realize that prunes don't have the best image – they are little less glamorous than figs and not quite as fashionable as dates – but *Prunes d'Agen* are a whole different matter. Jet black, squidgy and rich, these are considered such a delicacy that they even boast their own annual festival, the *Foire aux Pruneaux*.

Makes 1 large jar
Preparation time: 5 minutes
Cooking time: 30 minutes

500g pitted *Prunes d'Agen*

50ml Cognac or Armagnac

500ml water

4 tbsp sugar

1 cinnamon stick

1 star anise

a pinch of salt

2 oranges, zest of 1 and both peeled and sliced into rounds

Place all the ingredients, except the orange slices, in a saucepan and cover with the lid. Gently simmer over a low to medium heat for 30 minutes, then remove from the heat and leave to cool.

Arrange the orange slices on a serving platter with some of the cooled prunes alongside as a decadent dessert.

Les petites astuces – tips These prunes are very versatile and are great to have hanging around as a standby dessert. The syrupy juices can also double up as a sauce for ice cream.

Faire en avance – get ahead The prunes will keep well stored in an airtight jar or Tupperware in the fridge for up to a week.

Gateaux de la Dune du Pyla

SAND DUNE ICE-CREAM CAKES

Arcachon is postcard-pretty and boasts a very famous landmark: the largest sand dune in Europe, named the Dune du Pyla. It is sandwiched between the sweeping blue water of the Atlantic and a fragrant forest of pine trees. Inspired by the flavours and textures of this beautiful landscape, I snuck some pine nuts into the base of my recipe for ice-cream cake, made in tribute to the magnificent sand sculpture of Arcachon.

Serves 6

Preparation time: 1 hour • Resting time: 2 hours • Cooking time: 20 minutes
Equipment: an 8cm chef ring or biscuit cutter

60g seedless raisins • 45ml Sauternes wine or rum • 300g good-quality vanilla ice cream • *For the praline:* 75g caster sugar • 25ml water • 50g pine nuts • *For the biscuit base:* 100g butter • 75g light brown sugar • 1 egg, beaten • 100g self-raising white flour, sifted • *For the chocolate topping:* 300g white chocolate • 3 tbsp coconut oil

Soak the raisins in the alcohol for 2 hours, stirring every so often. To make the praline, line a baking tray with baking paper. Put the sugar and water in a large saucepan, heat gently until the sugar dissolves, then increase the heat to high. When the mixture starts to bubble and turns a caramel colour, add the pine nuts and swirl the pan around to coat them evenly. Pour on to the prepared tray and spread with a palette knife (be quick as it sets fast). Leave to cool then blitz in a food processor, or bash with the end of a rolling pin, until it has the texture of coarse breadcrumbs.

Preheat the oven to 170°C. Move the ice cream to the fridge. For the biscuit base, cream the butter with the sugar. Add the egg and mix well. Then stir in the flour and most of the praline (set aside a little for decoration). Line a 20cm x 26cm baking tray with baking paper and, using a spatula, spread the mixture on this until 1cm thick. Bake for 12–15 minutes or until nicely coloured. Using the chef ring or biscuit cutter, press out 6 rounds and set these aside to cool.

Mix the ice cream with the raisins (discarding any extra liquid) and, using a spoon and spatula, spread the mixture on to the biscuit base, building it up to a peak, so it looks like a little mountain. Smooth the edges with the spatula dipped in hot water. Freeze for 15 minutes until set firm.

Place the white chocolate and the coconut oil in a heatproof bowl over a pan of simmering water (make sure the bottom of the bowl doesn't touch the hot water). Melt and stir together, then remove from the heat. Take the ice-cream cakes out of the freezer, and ladle the melted topping over each one. Quickly sprinkle with a little of the remaining praline (the topping sets fast!) and either eat straight away or return to the freezer, where they will keep for a couple of months. Remove from the freezer 15 minutes before eating.

Crème brûlée á la semoule

SEMOLINA BURNT CREAMS

I love semolina pudding, but none of that hard stodgy stuff. I prefer creamy, smooth semolina (hence this being more of a cream than a pudding). There is something very comforting about savouring a little bowl of semolina, warm or cold, and at any time of the day for that matter. Sadly, for many people, semolina pudding brings back unpleasant memories of school canteens. So I've decided to give it a little French makeover, studding it with juicy sweet prunes and giving it a golden, crisp crème brûlée-style topping.

Serves 4
Preparation time: 15 minutes
Cooking time: 10 minutes
Resting time: at least 30 minutes

500ml almond milk or full-fat milk

35g semolina

4 ready-to-eat prunes, cut into very small pieces

4–6 tbsp sugar

Bring the milk to the boil in a saucepan. Add the semolina, then whisk hard for 5 minutes until the mixture has thickened. Remove from the heat, stir in the prunes, then divide evenly between 4 ramekins. Chill in the fridge for at least 30 minutes.

Just before serving, make the caramel topping. Sprinkle a nice even layer of sugar over each ramekin. Do this by holding the spoon at least 30cm above the ramekin (sprinkling from a height is the best way to create an even layer).

Place the ramekins on a metal tray. For best results, use a hand-held blowtorch. Holding it 10–12cm away from the sugar, move the flame slowly around the sugar, maintaining a steady, even motion. Stop torching just before the desired degree of caramel is reached, as the sugar will continue to cook for a few seconds after the flame has been removed.

If you don't have a blowtorch, take a large metal spoon and hold it in a gas flame until very hot (hold the handle with a tea towel or an oven glove to protect your hand). Carefully place the spoon on top of the sugar and move it around so that the heat from the spoon caramelizes the sugar.

Cannelés

Cannelés are to Bordeaux what *kouign-amann* is to Brittany: an iconic sweet of the region, which sees every patisserie and boulangerie striving to create the ultimate version. The batter is not dissimilar to that of a crêpe, but the quality varies wildly between pastry shops, as I discovered in my quest to find the best. Traditionally baked in a hot oven in scalloped copper moulds, *cannelés* caramelize and crisp on the outside, while the inside remains pale and airy. My recipe will have you producing perfect examples every time, even without the copper moulds.

Makes 14–16

Preparation time: 15 minutes

Resting time: 48 hours or up to 5 days

Cooking time: 1½ hours

Equipment: a silicone mould with 8 'lunch'-size cannelé holes or a muffin tin

500ml full-fat milk

50g unsalted butter, cubed

1 vanilla pod, split lengthways and seeds scraped out

100g plain white flour, sifted

250g icing sugar, sifted

1 tsp salt

2 eggs, plus 2 egg yolks

60ml rum

Put the milk and butter in a small saucepan with the vanilla pod and seeds. Bring to the boil over a medium heat, then remove from the heat and leave to cool a little.

Tip the flour, icing sugar and salt into a large bowl. In a separate bowl, lightly beat the eggs and yolks together.

When the milk has cooled, remove the vanilla pod and set aside. Pour the warm milk and eggs into the bowl containing the dry ingredients. Gently stir together until smooth (there may be a few lumps at this stage).

Strain the batter through a sieve into a clean bowl, pressing through the lumps until you have a smooth batter. Add the rum and stir until combined, then pop in the reserved vanilla pod. Cover with cling film and chill in the fridge for 2 days or longer – this will allow the flavours to infuse and will also relax the gluten resulting in a tender, less chewy *cannelé*. Try and remember to give it a stir every so often.

When you are ready to cook the *cannelé*, preheat the oven to 240°C. Heat the silicone mould in the oven for a couple of minutes then, using a small ladle, fill each hole four-fifths full with the batter.

Cook for 15 minutes, then reduce the heat to 190°C and cook for a further hour. Remove from the moulds and leave to cool on a wire rack. As they cool, the outside will develop a good crisp crust.

Cocktail au Lillet, gingembre et citron

LILLET, GINGER AND LEMON FIZZ

Lillet is an established favourite brand of aperitif founded in Bordeaux by the Lillet brothers. It's a blend of local Bordelais wine (Sauvignon Blanc, Semillon and Muscadelle for the white variety, and Cabernet Sauvignon and Merlot for the red) with a hint of citrus liqueur, which makes it very refreshing. It can be drunk on its own, well chilled, or, how I like it, with some tonic water and a hit of ginger.

Makes 1.5 litres
Preparation time: 15 minutes
Freezing time: 2 hours

500ml Lillet, or lemon vodka, well chilled

20g crystallized ginger, finely chopped

1 lemon, sliced

6 basil leaves

ice cubes

1 litre tonic water

_____

Une petite astuce – tip
To make a frozen cocktail, simply pour the mixture (without the ice cubes and lemon slices) into a large container. Place in the freezer for 2 hours or until frozen around the edges. Use a fork to break up the ice crystals every 30 minutes. Repeat this several times before serving with lemon slices.

Mix together the Lillet with the ginger, lemon, basil leaves and ice cubes. Top up with the tonic water (or leave out if you prefer).

Basque

LA MORUE

PORRU

LES CERISES NOIRES

LE PORC PIE NOIR
DU PAYS BASQUE

LA VAGUE

OCÉAN ATLANTIQUE

CÔTE D'AGENT

LE BÉRET
BASQUE

LES PIMENTS
D'ESPELETTE

LE JAMBON
DE BAYONNE

LA PLANCHE À SURF

ANGLET
BAYONNE
BIARRITZ
BIDART
ST JEAN DE LUZ

HENDAYE

ESPELETTE
ITXASSOU

LE PAYS BASQUE
(côte FRANCE)

LIMOI

LES PINXTOS

LES MOUCHOUS

LE GATEAU BASQUE

ESPAGNE

LE FROMAGE
DE BREBIS

LA PIPERADE

LES GUINDILLAS

SURFER'S PARADISE, PINTXOS PARTIES
AND BASQUE KISSES

It was an early touchdown in Biarritz. Although only an hour and 20 minutes by air from Paris down to this nook on the Atlantic coast, at first glance the Pays Basque seems a world apart. It was mid-autumn, the rain was pelting down and at 8 a.m. it was still dark and blustery. I headed off to roam the deserted streets of Biarritz in search of a hot drink and a sweet little something to keep me going on my explorations. From the ocean-facing windows at the historic pastel *patisserie*, Miremont, the day lightened to reveal an exceptional view of the craggy coastline, an odd surfer or two bravely bobbing in the water.

Biarritz feels quite literally exposed to the whims of weather. The waves crashed over the promenade, palm trees leant at 45 degrees and the gothic cathedral looked all the more imposing with swollen grey clouds clustering above it. But it is not just the landscape and exposure to the Atlantic that sets this part of extreme southwest France apart; the Pays Basque is one of the most unusual and unique regions I visited.

The Pays Basque was once part of the kingdom of Navarre, united with the Spanish part of the Basque region before it was split in the sixteenth century. This slight sense of segregation from the rest of France can still be felt, with various iconic symbols like the black basque beret and flag, as well as road signs in both French and Basque dialect.

When it comes to the food culture, that's where things really start to get interesting (read: confusing). *Pintxos (*see page 104*)*, Espelette pepper, hanging legs of cured hams and *planchas* are fundamental to the way the Basque French eat; items that rarely make a significant appearance in the rest of the country, being more closely associated with their Spanish neighbours.

Surprisingly for a nation that snubs spicy food, here in Biarritz – and even more so in the nearby village of Espelette – hot plump red chillies reign supreme. Heading inland, the road to Espelette takes you up and down and into the mist-shrouded lush green Basque hills. Farmhouses and sheep dot the countryside before Espelette appears before you with its bright white houses with fire engine red timber frames. The village's sole *raison d'etre* seems to be tourism associated to the great *piment d'Espelette*, which is not a bad thing. Strings of *piments* (Espelette peppers) hang everywhere: on hotels, houses, shop fronts, even the local Spar. They make *gelée d'Espelette* (lovely topped with a little *brebis* cheese, see page 127), Espelette salt, purée, paste, lollipops – you name it. They even rub their hams with it during the curing process.

Among Basque's other idiosyncrasies are its eating habits or, more specifically, *pintxos* hour. If ever a mealtime reflected a cultural attitude as a whole, this is it. Next to Biarritz's Les Halles (the famous food market) lies Bar Jean, a bustling establishment with young and old crammed in together, plates of *pintxos* piled high on the bar. The atmosphere is homely, laid back and welcoming; there is no room for Paris pretentions or menu rigidity here; I was determined to recreate this *pintxos* spirit in a party at home (see pages 104–9).

Bayonne is a short 8km drive from Biarritz, and is spectacularly set on the Nive river. The town is postcard-pretty, particularly in contrast to Biarritz's modern seaside resort architecture, with old higgledy-piggledy housing lining the river, all accessorized with different coloured shutters.

Les Halles, the covered market, was filled with butchers, fishmongers, grocers and bakers. However, it was the outside market that caught my eye. It was a joy to behold. Producers from the region lined the river showcasing fresh cèpes, knobbly squash and gnarly tomatoes, and those ever-present *piment d'Espelette* peppers in little woven baskets. Most of the market stands were tiny enterprises, one lady selling only 3kg bags of dinky little apples for two euros a pop.

It was in this region that I discovered the French penchant for the bacon sandwich. A *ventreche baguette*, with slices of bacon cooked on the plancha, piled into a baguette (see page 125). Perhaps we aren't so different from our Gallic neighbours after all.

The Pays Basque is famous for an eclectic variety of sweet stuffs, amongst them the Mouchous ('little kiss'), Gateau Basque (a controversial cake that we made at Le Cordon Bleu and not to everyone's taste) and chocolates. Macarons, like other things in the Pays Basque, are not as we know them. These are single layered, ganache free, rough and jagged like the Atlantic coast, but moist and chewy inside.

The Basque region is full of surprises, from its pervasive laidback surfer vibe and social style of eating, with its punchy seasonings and Spanish similarities. With a little help from Espelette peppers, you can create some punchy condiments to spice up your store cupboard and bring that edgy Basque style into your cooking.

Pintxos salés à la Française

FRENCH SAVOURY PINTXOS

Think *pintxos* and think Spanish tapas bar, a bustling help-yourself affair with high piles of nibbles impaled with sticks. Spanish and French cultures collide in the Basque region of France, where you are just as likely to find these delights as you are in San Sebastian, the home par excellence of the *pintxo*. Close to Les Halles, in Biarritz, I encountered an exemplary collection at Bar Jean, where groups of locals, young and old, were gathered at the bar, loading up their plates with a colourful array of these (mostly!) bite-sized goodies. These are the ultimate party snacks: cooler than canapés, colourful and quick to prepare, they are perfect for crowds and pretty much the easiest thing you can make for a drinks party. At their simplest, they are just a question of artistic assembly. All you need to do is raid your local deli counter and start skewering. Here is a selection of ingredients worth stocking up on for your savoury *pintxo* party:

thin slices of Bayonne ham (or prosciutto di Parma, San Daniele, Serrano), chunks of chorizo or other cured meats • cheeses: feta, Cheddar, mozzarella bocconcini, Roquefort, Gruyère • quail eggs (boil them for 2–2½ minutes) • cherry tomatoes • pickled mild chillies (often called *guindillas*) • olives (pitted, for practical purposes) • anchovies (pickled or jarred/tinned both have their merits) • a fresh baguette, cut into slices • cornichons, caperberries or gherkins • pickled beetroot and onions • jarred artichokes, mushrooms, roasted red peppers or other grilled antipasti • cocktail sticks or wooden skewers (these can be snipped in half with scissors to shorten)

Thread three or four different ingredients on to each cocktail stick or skewer. Get creative and allow for about 8–10 pintxos per person. The following ideas are my favourite combinations. They all make 8, and take about 10 minutes to prepare.

BASQUE FLAG ON A STICK

8 pickled cocktail onions, drained • 8 pickled green peppers • 8 semi-dried tomatoes

Thread one of each of the ingredients on to a cocktail stick. Repeat until you have used up all the ingredients.

BAKED FIGS WITH WALNUTS AND CHEESE

8 ripe figs • 8 cubes of goat's cheese (approx. 60g) • 8 walnut halves, roughly chopped • 1 tbsp runny honey

Preheat the oven to 160°C. Line a baking tray with foil and pop the figs on top. Cut a cross into the top of each fig, push a cube of goat's cheese into each one and sprinkle with walnuts. Bake for 10 minutes or until the cheese is bubbly. Drizzle a little runny honey on each fig before serving.

HAM AND COURGETTE RIBBONS WITH MELON

1 courgette • ¼ of a cantaloupe melon, deseeded • 4 slices of Bayonne ham, prosciutto di Parma or Serrano

Top and tail the courgette then run a peeler down the length of it to create 8 thin ribbons. Set aside. Using a melon-baller, if you have one, scoop out 8 balls of melon flesh or use a knife to cut 8 equal-sized cubes, about 3cm x 3cm. Cut the slices of ham in half lengthways. Pop a cocktail stick into the melon, then thread the ham in a ribbon on top and follow with the courgette ribbon. Repeat with the remaining ingredients.

TUNA AND CRÈME FRAÎCHE BITES

4 tbsp crème fraîche • 5 tbsp finely chopped cornichons, plus 8 little sliced rounds for garnish • 1 tsp Dijon mustard • a good pinch of sea salt • 8 thin rounds of baguette • 1 tin of good-quality tuna in spring water, drained (drained weight approx. 160g)

Mix together the crème fraîche, chopped cornichons, mustard and salt. Roughly spread the mixture over the slices of baguette and top each one with a generous chunk of tuna. Add a round of cornichon and secure the whole lot with a cocktail stick through the top.

LITTLE GEMS WITH MUSTARD VINAIGRETTE AND GRUYÈRE

2 Little Gem lettuces • 2 tbsp grainy mustard • 3 tbsp extra virgin olive oil • 100g mature Gruyère or Comté cheese, cut into slices, or 8 thin slices of Bayonne ham

Remove the outer leaves from the lettuces. Trim the bottoms and cut both Gems into quarters, lengthways. Rinse and pat dry with kitchen towel. Mix the mustard with the oil and brush on to the cut sides of the lettuce quarters. Place a slice of cheese on top of each and secure with a cocktail stick. For a carnivorous variation, wrap a slice of Bayonne ham around each quarter and secure with a cocktail stick.

SPICED OCTOPUS AND TOMATO CONCASSÉ

250g cooked octopus, roughly chopped • 2 tbsp extra virgin olive oil • a pinch of salt • ½ tsp Espelette pepper • ½ tsp paprika • 2 large tomatoes • 8 rounds of fresh baguette, about 2cm thick • a couple of sprigs of fresh chives, finely chopped

In a bowl mix together the octopus, oil, salt, pepper and paprika. Set aside. Bring a small pan of water to the boil (enough to cover the tomatoes). With a small knife, score the bottom of each tomato with a cross. Plunge the tomatoes into the boiling water for 10 seconds or until the skin begins to blister. Remove and plunge into a bowl of very cold water. Peel off the skin and cut each tomato in half crossways. Scoop out the seeds and chop the flesh into small cubes. Add the cubes to the bowl with the octopus and mix together. Divide the mixture evenly between the slices of bread and garnish with the chopped chives.

Baked figs with walnuts and cheese
& Tuna and crème fraîche bites

Basque flag on a stick

Little Gems with mustard vinaigrette and Gruyère

Spiced octopus and tomato concassé

Ham and courgette ribbons with melon

Cherry jam Lamingtons

Fresh fruit with chocolate dipping sauce
& Date and marzipan rolls

Frozen chocolate banana pops

Chocolate and cream buns &
Roasted pineapple, pistachio and mint

Pintxos sucrés à la Française

FRENCH SWEET PINTXOS

As with the savoury pintxo party, here is a selection of ingredients worth stocking up on for your sweet pintxos:

good-quality dark chocolate • different kinds of fresh berries: strawberries, raspberries, blackberries • Madeira or sponge loaf cake • chunks of bananas and pineapple • brioche buns • crème fraîche • dried fruit: apricots, figs, dates • nuts • chestnut spread • jam • peanut butter

The following recipe ideas are my favourite flavour combinations but feel free to make up some of your own. They all make 8, apart from the Roasted Pinapple, Pistachio and Mint *pintxo*, which makes 16. They each take about 10 minutes to prepare, but the Banana Pops need an hour in the freezer.

FROZEN CHOCOLATE BANANA POPS

4 bananas • 200g chocolate, broken into even pieces • 75g shelled hazelnuts, roasted and finely chopped

Line a large Tupperware with baking paper. Peel the bananas and cut in half to make 8 short pieces. Carefully insert a wooden skewer (trimmed if necessary) into the cut end of each banana, up to the tip without pushing it all the way through. Arrange the bananas on the baking paper and freeze for about an hour, until firm but not frozen hard.

In the meantime, melt the chocolate in a deep bowl set over a pan of simmering water, stirring occasionally, until smooth (make sure the bowl doesn't touch the hot water). Remove the bowl of chocolate from the pan and dunk one banana at a time into the chocolate, coating evenly. Sprinkle the hazelnuts over the banana while the chocolate is still wet, then return the coated banana to the baking paper-lined Tupperware while you cover the remaining bananas. Pop the bananas back into the freezer to firm up the chocolate, then serve.

CHERRY JAM LAMINGTONS

250g best-quality Madeira cake • 100g smooth cherry jam • 8 tbsp desiccated coconut, toasted

Cut the cake lengthways into slices about 1.5cm thick, then cut 3cm squares from those slices to end up with 16 evenly sized pieces of cake. Using a teaspoon, coat each side of the squares of cake with jam and sandwich two pieces together. Toss in the coconut, securing with a cocktail stick through the centre. Repeat with the remaining 14 squares to make 7 more Lamingtons.

FRESH FRUIT WITH CHOCOLATE DIPPING SAUCE

8 strawberries, hulled • 8 blackberries • 1 kiwi, peeled and cut into 8 chunks • optional: 8 Madeira cake squares, roughly 3cm x 3cm • 100g plain or milk chocolate • 150g double cream

Divide the fruits and cake squares, if using, on to cocktail sticks or skewers. Chop the chocolate into small pieces. Heat the double cream in a saucepan over a medium heat, stirring to avoid it burning. When it starts to bubble, pour over the chocolate. Leave for a few seconds and then stir the two together to form a luscious thick sauce. Serve in a little pot next to the skewers for dipping.

DATE AND MARZIPAN ROLLS

8 firm, dry dates • 120g marzipan • optional: 8 crystallized rose petals

Slice the dates in half lengthways and remove the stone. Align the halves lengthways, head-to-tail, on a piece of baking paper, overlapping the tip slightly. Fold the baking paper over and, using a rolling pin, flatten out the date to a thickness of about 4mm and roughly 8cm long. Cut the marzipan into 8 pieces and roll each piece to the same shape as the date. Place a piece on top of a date and roll it up. If using a rose petal, place on top and secure with a cocktail stick. Repeat with the remaining dates.

ROASTED PINEAPPLE, PISTACHIO AND MINT

1 small pineapple • 4 tsp Demerara sugar • 3 tbsp finely chopped pistachios • 16 small mint leaves

Preheat the oven to 200˚C. Line a roasting tray with baking paper. Peel the pineapple and cut it in half across the middle, then cut into quarters, lengthways. Trim out the tough internal core. Place in the roasting tray and toss the segments in the sugar. Bake for 8–10 minutes or until lightly caramelized. Remove from the oven and cut each quarter into 4 chunks. Cover half of the pineapple pieces in pistachios. Skewer a piece of coated pineapple with a cocktail stick, add a mint leaf, then add a piece of uncoated pineapple.

CHOCOLATE AND CREAM BUNS

4 small finger brioche rolls • 8 tbsp full-fat crème fraîche • sea salt, for sprinkling • 16 squares of good-quality dark chocolate or 8 tbsp chocolate chips

Cut each brioche roll in half lengthways. Spread 2 tablespoons of the crème fraîche on the bottom half of each roll and sprinkle with a pinch of sea salt. Place 4 squares of chocolate or half a tablespoon of chocolate chips on each bun to cover the base. Then pop on the lid of the roll to make a sandwich. Place a griddle pan over a medium heat. When the pan is warm, add the rolls. Use a spatula to press the rolls on to the pan to get nice griddle marks. Turn over after about 45 seconds and cook on the other side. Cut each one in half, and secure with a cocktail stick. Serve warm.

Sauce xipister

XIPISTER SAUCE

Every restaurant, bistro or Basque household has a version of xipister sauce. There's no real secret; it's just about making use of the products in the region, combined to create a quintessential condiment. It's the Basque answer to our Worcestershire sauce or Japan's soy sauce. Don't be shy using the xipister; it adds a little lift to pretty much any savoury dish and is great drizzled on meat, fish or even pizza. It's also good used as a vinaigrette on salad. The quality of your sauce will depend on the quality of the vinegar and olive oil you use.

Preparation time: 10 minutes
Resting time: at least 1 week
Equipment: a 500ml glass bottle or jar with a lid

300ml white wine vinegar or cider vinegar

150ml extra virgin olive oil

1 Espelette pepper or 1 medium hot chilli, washed and halved lengthways

2 cloves of garlic, peeled and squashed using the back of a knife

1 bay leaf

1 sprig of fresh rosemary

2 sprigs of fresh thyme

zest of 1 lemon

Place all the ingredients in the glass bottle or jar, put the lid on and shake well. Leave in a cool place for at least a week. Shake well again before using. The taste will get stronger the longer the ingredients are left to marinate. The sauce will keep in an airtight bottle or jar in a cool, dark place for a couple of months.

Piquillos farcis à la morue

PIQUILLOS PEPPERS STUFFED WITH COD

This Basque dish is as a traditional as it gets. Delicious sweet little pickled peppers stuffed with a lovely salt cod concoction. Salt cod, or *bakailao* in Basque, is traditionally used. It's hugely popular in Spain and parts of France and is essentially a method of drying and salting cod to preserve it. If you track down salt cod for this recipe, rehydrate it in milk or water for 24 hours before rinsing and patting dry. Otherwise use any cooked white fish.

Serves 4 as a main course
Preparation time: 10 minutes
Cooking time: 10 minutes

2 red onions, peeled and
finely chopped

4 cloves of garlic, peeled and
finely minced

½ tsp Espelette pepper (or more if
you like it hotter)

1 tbsp olive oil, plus a little extra
to drizzle

200g rehydrated salt cod, fresh
cod fillet, pollock, coley or black
bream, flaked

juice of ½ a lemon

2 tbsp finely chopped fresh parsley

salt (only if not using salt cod)

12 piquillos peppers (from a jar or tin),
at room temperature

optional: Xipister sauce (see page 112)

Fry the onion, garlic and Espelette pepper in the oil until golden. Add the flaked fish and cook for a further couple of minutes. Add the lemon juice and half the parsley. Stir together and cook until the lemon juice has evaporated. Taste for seasoning and add more Espelette pepper if you like it a little spicier.

Carefully open up each piquillos pepper and fill with the fish stuffing. Drizzle with a little more oil or Xipister sauce and garnish with the rest of the parsley. Eat warm.

Plate hunting at a flea market in Bordeaux.

Tartines de tomates avec des rillettes de sardines

TOMATO SLICES WITH SARDINE PÂTÉ

Fresh sardines are abundant in the markets of Biarritz, so it's only natural to find them in many forms on menus in the local cafés, bistros and restaurants. This recipe makes the most of the preserved kind, the best of which you'll find labelled as pilchards. Don't dismiss a tinned sardine, as paying the price makes all the difference. There shouldn't be more than two ingredients on the label: sardines and olive oil. Traditionally, *rillettes,* a rough pâté, are served with crusty bread or toast but tomatoes make a delicious gluten-free alternative!

Serves 4 as a starter or light snack
Preparation time: 15 minutes
Cooking time: 2 minutes

1 tbsp olive oil

3 or 4 different coloured firm tomatoes, cut into 1.5cm slices

For the sardine pâté

100g cream cheese

1 shallot, peeled and finely chopped

1 tbsp finely chopped capers

2 tbsp finely chopped fresh flat-leaf parsley

1 tsp lemon juice

zest of ½ a lemon

a pinch of Espelette pepper

sea salt

1 tin of good-quality sardines or pilchards in olive oil (drained weight 100g), large bones removed

Mix together all the ingredients for the pâté apart from the sardines (reserving some of the parsley for a garnish) and season with sea salt.

Drain the sardines, saving some of the oil to drizzle on top. Use a fork to mash the fish until you have a chunky texture and then stir into the cream cheese mixture.

Heat a large non-stick pan with the tablespoon of olive oil over a high heat. When the pan is hot add the tomato slices. Cook for a minute on each side or until caramelized. Make sure not to overcook them, or they will become soft.

Serve a dollop of the pâté on top of each of the tomato slices, sprinkle with the reserved parsley and drizzle with a little of the sardine oil.

Une petite astuce – tip Choose firm, not overly ripe tomatoes that aren't watery otherwise, when you come to cook them, they will become mushy and disintegrate.

Faire en avance – get ahead The rillettes will keep in the fridge in an airtight container for several days. You may need to use a fork to fluff the mixture, as it will start to set.

Porc et palourdes en cocotte

PORK AND CLAMS WITH CIDER AND BUTTER BEANS

The Basque coast is a surfers' paradise. The rocky, ragged coastline is punctuated with stretches of windswept beach, much more rough and ready than its Mediterranean counterpart. I've always been the envious surfer spectator, watching them gracefully (or not so gracefully, depending on their skill) catch and tame the waves whatever the weather. Surf 'n' turf is not what you would traditionally think of when it comes to Basque food but it's my homage to the Basque love of pork with some gems from the ocean: clams. The clams are thrown in right at the end, adding a lip-smacking saltiness to the broth.

Serves 4–6 as a main course
Preparation time: 25 minutes
Cooking time: 2–2½ hours

1 onion, peeled and finely chopped

3 cloves of garlic, peeled and squashed using the back of the knife

2 tbsp butter

1kg pork shoulder, tied

20g fresh flat-leaf parsley

375ml dry cider

4 tbsp cider vinegar

1 litre hot vegetable stock

4 bay leaves

2 sprigs of fresh thyme

4 small apples, peeled and cored

1 tbsp brown sugar

1 tsp sea salt

10 black peppercorns, crushed

1kg clams, cleaned

1 x 400g tin of haricot beans or butter beans (drained weight 230g), drained and rinsed

In a large pot with a lid fry the onion and garlic in the butter on a medium heat until translucent. Add the pork shoulder and fry on all sides until golden.

Tie a string around the parsley stalks to make a tight bundle. Cut off the leaves (save them for later) and add the stems to the pot with the cider, vinegar, hot stock, bay leaves, thyme, apples, sugar, salt and peppercorns. Bring to a gentle simmer and skim any scum that comes to the top using a slotted spoon. Simmer very gently for 2–2½ hours, until the meat is tender and falling apart.

Remove the meat from the pot, set aside in a tray and cover with foil. Leave to rest for 10 minutes. Pour the cooking liquid through a fine sieve into a bowl, discarding the strained bits. Rinse out the pot before pouring the cooking liquid back in. Bring to a boil and then add the clams and beans. Bring back to the boil and cook for a further 3 minutes with the lid on. Check that the clams are open and discard any that remain closed. Taste for seasoning.

Shred the pork meat using your fingers or a fork and serve with the clams, beans and broth. Sprinkle with the finely chopped parsley.

Une petite astuce – tip Any leftover pork will be delicious in a roll with a dollop of hot spicy mustard: the perfect post-surf snack.

Batons d'aubergines pimentées avec couscous

SPICY AUBERGINE CHIPS WITH COUSCOUS

On a visit to the Saturday market in Bayonne, a picturesque town just 20 minutes drive from Biarritz, I discovered lots of gnarly looking aubergines. But it wasn't just their gnarliness that captured my attention: some were a dark shade of purple, others pale cream, some were striped and others speckled. Short, fat and slightly misshapen, they are outcasts of the gastronomic world, those that never make it into our supermarkets. I threw them into my basket as soon as I spotted them then promptly headed back to the kitchen and conjured up this dish.

Serves 4 as a starter or 2 as a main course
Preparation time: 30 minutes
Cooking time: 30 minutes

2 cloves of garlic, peeled

a pinch of salt

2 tbsp olive oil

1 tbsp tomato paste

1 tsp Espelette pepper

2 medium aubergines

a handful of chopped parsley, to garnish

For the couscous

160g couscous

zest of 1 lemon

a pinch of salt

180ml boiling water

1 tsp extra virgin olive oil

For the yoghurt sauce

100g plain yoghurt

1 tbsp lemon juice

a pinch of salt

Preheat the oven to 180°C. Line a baking tray with baking paper. Pound the garlic with the salt in a pestle and mortar until it forms a smooth paste. Blend in the oil, tomato paste and Espelette pepper.

Cut the aubergines lengthways into 2cm-thick slices. Cut each slice into 2cm-wide strips to make long sticks. Throw away the spongy core. Brush the remaining batons with the spicy marinade. Place on the lined baking tray and cook in the oven for 30 minutes or until tender.

Meanwhile, place the couscous, lemon zest and salt in a large bowl and pour over the boiling water. Place a large plate on top of the bowl and leave to stand for 5 minutes. Drizzle with the oil and fluff up with a fork.

To make the yoghurt sauce, mix together all the ingredients and taste for seasoning.

Serve the cooked aubergines on a bed of couscous. Drizzle with the yoghurt sauce and sprinkle with some chopped parsley.

---

*Une petite astuce – **tip*** Pick aubergines that feel firm with a shiny skin.

*Faire en avance – **get ahead*** The marinade for the sauce can be made in advance and kept in an airtight container for a couple of days. The same goes for the yoghurt sauce.

Sandwich au ventreche et ketchup Basque

BACON AND BASQUE KETCHUP SARNIE

I spotted the locals in Biarritz gobbling down bacon sandwiches at a farming fair. It was the first time I had ever seen anybody in France eat bacon in such a quintessentially British way. I love sauce in my sandwich, especially when it packs a punch, so my version of ketchup is spicy, jammy and slightly sweet, which, without a doubt, works wonderfully with chips, chops, fried fish . . . you name it. This recipe makes roughly 450g of sauce, enough for many bacon sarnies, and will keep in sterilized bottles for up to six months.

Serves 4
Preparation time: 15 minutes
Cooking time: 40 minutes
Equipment: sterilized jars

For the Basque ketchup

1 tbsp olive oil

1 onion, peeled and finely sliced

5 cloves of garlic, peeled and crushed

3 bay leaves

1 Espelette pepper or a medium-hot chilli, stalk removed and roughly chopped

500g cherry tomatoes

1 peeled roasted red pepper from a jar (roughly 150g), chopped

175ml red wine vinegar

50g sugar

a pinch of salt, to taste

For the sandwich

4 rolls, or a large baguette, quartered

8 rindless rashers of back bacon

First make the ketchup. Heat the oil in a small saucepan over a medium heat and fry the onion with the garlic, bay leaves and Espelette pepper for about 10 minutes, until the onion begins to caramelize. Stir in the tomatoes and roasted pepper, cover with the lid and leave to simmer for 15 minutes.

Remove the bay leaves, pour the mixture into a blender and blitz until smooth. (At this point it would make a great pasta sauce.)

Pour the sauce back into the pan and add the vinegar and sugar. Taste and add salt if required. Cook, stirring continuously, over a medium to high heat for about 15 minutes, until the mixture reaches a ketchup consistency. Season, to taste.

Spoon the ketchup through a sterilized funnel into sterilized bottles, then seal tightly and place in a cool dark place or in the fridge until needed.

For the bacon sarnies, preheat the grill to medium-high. Place the rolls in the oven to warm. Arrange the bacon on a piece of foil on a baking tray and place under the grill. Cook for 5–6 minutes, until crisp, then turn the bacon over and cook on the other side for another minute or so.

Cut the rolls in half and spread generously with the ketchup. Top with two slices of bacon per roll.

Gelée de piment d'Espelette

ESPELETTE JELLY

A cupboard staple in any Basque kitchen, use it as you would use mustard. It goes especially well with cheese.

Makes: approx. 400g
Preparation time: 10 minutes
Cooking time: 25 minutes
Equipment: sterilized jars

30g Espelette peppers or medium-hot chillies

500ml white or red wine

approx. 300g sugar

15g pectin powder

Wash the peppers or chillies, remove and discard the stalks and chop the flesh finely. Place in a pan with their seeds and the wine. Bring to the boil and continue to boil for 10 minutes. Remove from the heat and leave to cool.

Strain the cooled mixture through a fine sieve into a clean saucepan. Weigh the liquid and add the same amount of sugar.

Add the pectin and bring to a boil while continually whisking. Boil for 3–5 minutes until it coats the back of the spoon. Pour into sterilized jars and seal tightly. The jelly will keep 6 months in a dark, cool cupboard. Once opened it should be stored in the fridge and used within 4 days.

Terrine aux cerises noires

BLACK CHERRY TERRINE

Itxassou, a village just inland from the Basque coast, is where most of the region's famed cherries are from. There are numerous varieties: Xapata is a yellow-orange colour and is the most acidic in taste, making it an excellent unadulterated, eating-straight-from-the-bag cherry; Peloa is a deep red cherry, generally eaten raw; and, finally Beltza, the most famous deep, dark cherries of the region with their natural sweetness, ideal for jam making. Traditional Basque cherry jam doesn't use pectin; instead the cherry stones are cracked and cooked with the fruit as they contain a natural gelling agent, which thickens the jam. This cherry terrine works as a dessert with whipped cream or vanilla ice cream but, as it's not overly sweet, it's equally delicious teamed with a creamy goat's cheese or slivers of cured meats.

Serves 6–8

Preparation time: 10 minutes
Cooking time: 15 minutes
Chilling time: 4 hours, or overnight

½ a vanilla pod, halved lengthways and seeds scraped

425g stoned jarred cherries, in their juices, or frozen cherries, defrosted

250ml water

40g sugar

a pinch of salt

4 leaves of gelatin (7g), soaked in water until soft

juice of 1 lemon

Line a 450g loaf tin with cling film or use an unlined Tupperware container.

Put the vanilla pod and seeds in a saucepan with the cherries and juice, water, sugar and salt. Heat over a medium heat, whisking or stirring until the sugar dissolves. Bring to the boil then take off the heat and leave to cool for 10 minutes.

Remove the vanilla pod. Squeeze the excess water from the gelatin and then whisk the gelatin into the cherry mixture. Once it has completely dissolved pour into the lined loaf tin or the Tupperware. Place in the fridge and leave to set for at least 4 hours or overnight.

When ready to serve, loosen the cling film from the edges of the loaf tin, place a plate on top and turn the whole thing upside down. Remove the cling film and cut into slices. If you're using an unlined Tupperware, dip the base in a bowl of hot water for a couple of seconds, place a plate on top and turn over; it should slip out easily.

Serving suggestions

Sweet: Whipped cream • Vanilla or dark-chocolate ice cream • Shortbread and a dollop of crème fraîche

Savoury: Creamy goat's cheese and endive salad • Rich or fatty meats, such as magret de canard and jambon

Beret Basque au chocolat

CHOCOLATE BASQUE BERET

The black beret is the sartorial symbol of the Basque region; so much so that they even named a chocolate cake after it. A classic butterless *genoise*, doused in syrup and encased in a simple chocolate ganache, this is a serious chocolate bomb of a beret.

Serves 8

Preparation time: 30 minutes
Cooking time: 18–24 minutes
Equipment: an 18cm round cake tin, at least 5cm deep, buttered

a knob of butter, softened for greasing

20g dark chocolate, frozen for decorating

For the chocolate genoise

120g sugar

4 eggs, at room temperature

120g plain white flour, sifted

20g cocoa powder, sifted

For the sugar syrup

50g sugar

50ml water

optional: 2 tbsp rum, kirsch, Cointreau or amaretto

For the chocolate ganache

200ml double cream

200g dark chocolate, finely chopped

a pinch of salt

a knob of butter

Preheat the oven to 160°C. Tip the sugar into a glass or metal bowl and crack in the eggs. Place the bowl over a pan of simmering water (making sure the bowl doesn't touch the hot water). Whisk the eggs and sugar with an electric whisk until very pale and almost tripled in size. This can take a while so be patient. Remove from the heat.

Mix the flour and cocoa powder together. Sift a third into the egg mixture and fold in very gently. Repeat with half the remaining mixture, and then again, until it is all incorporated. Do this very lightly and don't over-mix, or the resulting cake will be rubbery. Scrape into the prepared cake tin and cook in the oven for 18–24 minutes until a skewer inserted into the middle comes out clean. Turn the cake out on to a wire rack and leave to cool.

Meanwhile, put the sugar and water in a saucepan and bring to the boil. When the sugar has completely dissolved, remove from the heat and leave to cool, then stir in the rum, if using.

Bring the cream to the boil in a small pan. Pour over the finely chopped chocolate and salt and leave for 2 minutes before stirring together with the butter to a smooth chocolate mixture (don't over-stir, otherwise the ganache will become stiff).

When the cake has cooled, use a sharp knife to trim the side of it to form a dome, then cut it in half horizontally. Place the bottom layer on your serving plate. Brush very liberally with the sugar syrup and then, using a palette knife, spread with half of the ganache. Top with the other half of the cake and brush well with more sugar syrup. Spread ganache all over the cake, smoothing it out. Decorate with grated or shaved frozen chocolate and a piece of candied orange.

Crème au chocolat noir

DARK CHOCOLATE PUDDING

Chocolate has a long history in the Basque region since the Jews, fleeing persecution in Portugal, first introduced it to Bayonne in 1609. By the nineteenth century, chocolate had become so popular that Bayonne boasted 33 chocolate ateliers with over 130 chocolate masters. This chocolate pudding is rich and unctuous, but its richness is offset by the crème fraîche. It is delicious hot or cold.

Serves 6
Preparation time: 15 minutes
Cooking time: 15 minutes

10g cornflour

50g golden caster sugar

200ml whole milk

100ml double cream

85g good quality dark chocolate, finely grated or chopped

a knob of butter, softened

crème fraîche, to serve

optional: a pinch of Espelette pepper

Put the cornflour, sugar, milk and cream in a small pot. Place over a medium heat and whisk continuously for about 4 minutes until thickened. When it releases a bubble or two, remove from the heat and whisk in the chocolate and the butter. Divide between ramekins or glasses and serve with crème fraîche and sprinkle with Espelette pepper.

Les petites astuces – tips Use a dark chocolate (around 70 per cent cocoa) for this recipe. Anything less won't give this pudding its rich chocolatey flavour. And make sure to chop the chocolate finely. If the chunks are too big, they won't melt and your puds will end up lumpy.

Don't leave the mixture to stand after cooking. Immediately divide it between the ramekins otherwise lumps may form.

Bisous Chaumontais

CHAUMONTAIS KISSES

This recipe is the precious little offspring of a marriage between a *muxus*, a moist almond macaroon sandwich meaning 'kiss' in the local dialect, and a *Chaumontais*, a pastry made from cloudlike meringue with a golden hazelnut cream filling. While they were both a delight to eat on my visit to the Basque region, the *muxus* could have benefitted from the traditional Parisian ganache filling, and the *Chaumontais* were exceptionally enormous. So I thought I'd add a little Parisian finesse to these two classics and create dainty meringues with praline cream, easy to pop in your mouth and utterly moreish. Just like kisses, you can't get enough of them.

Makes approx. 30 kisses
Preparation time: 30 minutes
Cooking time: 2 hours

2 egg whites

several drops of lemon juice

100g sugar

1 x praline recipe (see page 276)

100g butter, softened

First make the praline (see page 276). Preheat the oven to 80°C. Whisk the egg whites in a clean glass or metal bowl and when they begin to froth, add a few drops of lemon juice plus a couple of tablespoons of the sugar. Continue to whisk for a further minute before adding a little more sugar. Repeat until all the sugar is used and the egg whites are stiff. Scrape into a piping bag or freezer bag and snip off the corner.

Line a large baking tray with baking paper. Pipe a dot of meringue under each corner to keep the paper in place then pipe ten-pence-sized dollops of meringue across the paper, leaving a gap between each one. Sprinkle a little praline on top of each meringue then place in the middle of the oven and bake for 1½ hours. Leave in the oven with the door ajar for 30 minutes before removing from the oven and leaving to cool completely on the tray.

Whip the butter until pale white before mixing in the praline (keeping back 2 heaped tablespoons). Spread a small blob on to a meringue before sandwiching with another meringue. Once the meringues are sandwiched together, roll them in the remaining praline so it sticks to the outer edge of the filling.

Provence

LE MIEL
LES ABEILLES
LA LAVANDE
LE CHEVAL DE CAMARGUE
LE RIZ ROUGE DE CAMARGUE
LE FLAMANT DE CAMARGUE
LE ROSÉ
LE SAVON DE MARSEILLE
LES NAVETTES
LA SARDINE
LES COQUELICOTS
LES CALISSONS
LE NOUGAT DE MONTÉLIMAR
LE TOURNESOL
LES OLIVES NIÇOISE
LES AGRUMES DE MENTON
LES CYPRES

BRIANÇON
GAP
PROVENCE
ORANGE
AVIGNON
MONT VENTOUX
LUBERON
CARMAGUE
AIX EN PROVENCE
MARSEILLE
GRASSE
NICE MENTON
CANNES
ST TROPEZ
TOULON
CÔTE D'AZUR

MER MÉDITERRANÉE

THE MENACING MISTRAL, FRAGRANT HERBS AND ALFRESCO DINING

Heading down on the train from Paris to Nice at the beginning of November, the colours of the landscape changed from urban greys and cold blues to warm countryside browns and oranges before turning a dry, hot yellow with sparse patches of green. Once the train reached Marseille it hugged the coastline, whizzing through St Tropez and then Cannes, revealing glimpses of azur blue sea and palm trees, and finally arriving at Nice.

Nice was nice (with such a name it had to be) but I was more interested in visiting the olive growers in the hills behind the city. I hopped in my little hire car and drove off up the winding roads and down the narrow dirt tracks, often so tight that you had to honk your horn before going round a bend. I finally reached my destination: a wide expanse of luscious trees laden with ripe black olives. The Nice olive is not particularly big but that doesn't mean it lacks punch. Considering its petite size it has a bold peppery and fruity taste. The Nice olive boasts an AOC label, meaning it's protected against imposters and local quality is fiercely maintained. Hence the olive oils and tapenades made using Nice olives are completely different to their Spanish or Italian counterparts, making them a little bit of a delicacy.

A beautiful drive along the coast further east of Nice (I just needed a vintage car, headscarf and sunglasses and I could have been starring in a movie from the 1950s) is the little town of Menton, on the border with Italy. Don't be surprised if you hear the locals speaking Italian as well as French at the market (Italians often do their grocery shopping in Menton, and vice versa). Menton has the perfect climate for citrus fruits, and lemons and oranges were just coming into season when I visited. The lemons are transformed into various products here: preserves, oils, mustards, savoury spreads, liquor, perfume, soaps . . . this humble citrus fruit has rightly become a star of the tourist trade.

My second trip to the south didn't boast the stereotypical sunshine, but the famously ferocious Mistral wind made itself known, howling at 130kph around Marseille. I took shelter in the oldest homewares store in France, *La Maison d'Empereur*, which has been in business since 1827. It was a treasure trove of kitchen pots, pans and gadgets: a true cook's paradise. A couple of minutes' walk away is the *vieux port*, the old harbour, where, when the weather is good, the fishermen (and women) rock up with their boats, tip out their catch and sell it on the shore. There were plenty of little sardines to be spotted, although not one big enough to block the port, as the old story goes. In the eighteenth century, a large ship, *La Sartine*, was attacked near Marseille. Although badly damaged, the boat managed to sail into the harbour, where it promptly sank, blocking the harbour mouth so that no boats could go in or out. This had a devastating effect on people living there and the story spread throughout France. However, in its retelling, the ship changed from *Sartine* to *Sardine,* and postcards and posters depicting the Marseillais hauling a gigantic sardine from the port can still be spotted at antique markets and shops.

Marseille is unlike the rest of Provence and has more similarities with Paris. It has a dynamic cosmopolitan feel, thanks to its creative scene and the diverse range of ethnic groups calling the city home. The North African influence can certainly be felt, with numerous shops selling ingredients and homewares and a volume of restaurants specializing in spices, tagines, couscous and sweet pastries. Heading inland provides quite the contrast. Here, the landscape still looks very much as it was depicted in the famous Provençal ochre, rosé pink and lavender coloured landscapes painted over a hundred years ago.

Just as the North African spices, such as harissa and *ras el hanout*, spike the air in certain neighbourhoods in Marseille, the fragrant aroma of thyme and lavender greets you when you walk through the fields of Provence, brushing your legs against the wild flowering herbs. The range of different flowers provides an excellent food source for bees, and, as a result, Provence has a rich variety of honeys, with lavender honey being the most well known. Beehives are moved around during the warmer months to produce different types of honey.

When the menacing Mistral wind has died down, sitting outside and enjoying a glass of chilled rosé could not be more fitting. To accompany the wine, food tends to be simple, with plenty of vegetables on the table (unlike the rest of France); a simply baked tian (see page 166), stuffed *petits farcis* (see page 144) or a colourful salad with fish (see page 151).

The flavours of Provence truly sum up the taste of summer for me. The fragrant aromas of the famous blend of Provençal herbs, colourful vegetables, a crisp refreshing glass of rosé . . . all best enjoyed outside. Even if the weather doesn't permit *al fresco* eating, you can still enjoy a little bit of Provence on your plate with this collection of recipes.

Ribs aux cassis avec couscous à la menthe et fèves

STICKY CASSIS PORK RIBS WITH MINT AND BROAD BEAN COUSCOUS

When I was a kid I would often make myself a blackcurrant drink after school (usually with more cordial than Mum would like). Little did I know that I would be doing that when I was a grown-up, too. A dash of almost black, glistening crème de cassis with some Champagne and you have yourself a delicious Kir Royale (or just Kir when paired with white wine). A very refreshing way to unwind after a long day. But it turns out it needn't be confined to the liquor cabinet. In a moment of inspiration, I reached for the crème de cassis thinking it would be perfect for making a sticky glaze for some pork ribs and, lo and behold, it was.

Serves 4–6

Preparation time: 30 minutes
Resting time: 1 hour, or overnight
Cooking time: 2½ hours

160g blackcurrant jam

4 tbsp runny honey

125ml crème de cassis

1 tsp freshly ground pepper

1 lemon, zested and roughly chopped

salt

1.5kg pork ribs or beef short ribs

For the couscous

20g fresh mint, leaves and stalk separated

200g fresh or frozen broad beans

425ml boiling water

200g couscous

2 tbsp olive oil

Whisk together the jam, honey, crème de cassis, pepper, lemon zest and 2 teaspoons of salt. Place the ribs and chopped lemon with the marinade in a large freezer bag and seal it tightly. Give it a shake so the ribs are covered and then leave to marinate in the fridge for at least an hour, but preferably overnight.

Preheat the oven to 150°C. Place the ribs, chopped lemon and the marinade in a large tray, cover with foil and cook for 2 hours. Turn the heat up to 200°C, remove the foil and baste the ribs with the marinade. Roast for another 15–30 minutes, basting a couple of times. The sauce should become sticky and thick and the ribs should be dark and glossy from the sauce. Remove from the oven, transfer the ribs to a dish and cover with foil. Pour the sauce into a saucepan and boil for 5–10 minutes then pour the reduced sauce over the ribs.

Meanwhile, make the couscous. Roughly chop the mint stalks and place in a pot with the broad beans, a pinch of salt and the boiling water. Bring to a boil and then pour over the couscous. Cover with cling film or a clean tea towel and leave to stand for 10 minutes. Remove the mint stalks and fluff up with a fork, then stir in the mint leaves, oil and taste for salt. Serve with the sticky ribs.

Alfresco eating Provence-style

Rouleaux Niçois

CANNELLONI NIÇOISE-STYLE

The French Mediterranean coast is the blessed land of the olive. I visited several olive producers around Nice. One of them, Champs Soleil, stood out in my memory not only for their fantastic olives but also for the different vegetables they grow organically: aubergines, peppers, tomatoes, courgettes. They then combine the olives with the other vegetables to produce a range of tapenades that really capture the sunshine-ripened flavours of Nice in a jar. These flavours are all packed into this recipe: black olive tapenade, grilled red peppers, courgette ribbons and tomatoes. You might begrudge the use of pasta in a Franco-centric cookbook, but this is where France and Italy meet, and, despite their intrinsically stubborn nature, the French love a bit of pasta.

Serves 4 as a main course
Preparation time: 25 minutes
Cooking time: 20 minutes

For the cherry tomato sauce

500g cherry tomatoes, halved

1 tbsp olive oil

a pinch of salt

For the filling

2 courgettes

8 large sheets of fresh lasagne (16cm x 22cm)

8 tsp black olive tapenade or paste

200g grilled red peppers (from a jar), drained and roughly chopped

200g cooked artichokes, roughly chopped

freshly ground pepper

200g crème fraîche

1 small handful of fresh flat-leaf parsley leaves

finely grated zest and juice of ½ a lemon

Preheat the oven to 180°C. Pop the tomatoes, oil and salt in a small saucepan. Cover with the lid and cook over a medium heat for 8 minutes or until the tomatoes have burst and become mushy. Meanwhile, top and tail the courgettes and, using a speed peeler, make long ribbons. Stop when you get to the spongy seed core, and discard.

With the lasagne sheets laid portrait, spread the tapenade thinly over them. Lay a few of the courgette ribbons down the length of the sheets to just cover each sheet in a thin layer. Mix together the peppers and artichokes and spoon 3 tablespoons of the mixture down the centre of each of the sheets, then roll up tightly from the long side to make a roll, trapping the filling in the centre. Place in a baking dish. Repeat with the other sheets of lasagne.

Pour the tomatoes over the lasagne rolls. Stir some pepper into the crème fraîche until smooth and dollop randomly over the top. Cook for about 30 minutes, until golden and bubbly.

Chop the flat-leaf parsley finely with the lemon zest. Scatter over the cooked pasta and squeeze over the lemon juice just before serving. Serve with a green salad.

---

*Les petites astuces – **tips*** If your lasagne sheets are a little dry, pop them in a bowl of boiling water for 30 seconds or so. When they are supple, drain them and pat dry with kitchen towel or a clean tea towel.

Les petits légumes farcis aux herbes de Provence

VEGETABLES STUFFED WITH RED RICE
AND HERBES DE PROVENCE

When it comes to seasonings, nothing could be more quintessentially Provençal than *herbes de Provence*. Made up of savory, fennel, basil, thyme and sometimes lavender, this fragrant blend works delightfully well sprinkled over vegetables and grilled meats, adding a little taste of the sunny south to the everyday. Camargue red rice is another of my favourite ingredients from Provence. It holds it shape and bite, adding an earthy nuttiness to whatever dish it graces. *Les petits farcis* is a popular Provençal dish of stuffed mixed Mediterranean vegetables. It originated as a way of using up leftovers.

Serves 4–6
Preparation time: 15 minutes
Cooking time: 45 minutes

150g red rice

4 large beef or plum tomatoes

4 round courgettes*

4 small red or yellow peppers

4 tbsp extra virgin olive oil

salt and freshly ground pepper

1 red onion, peeled and
finely chopped

2–4 large mushrooms
(approx. 125g), wiped

10 cherry tomatoes, roughly chopped

10 olives, pitted

1 tbsp chopped capers, drained

optional: 40g raisins, soaked in warm water for 5 minutes and drained

2 tbsp dried *herbes de Provence* or a mixture of fresh herbs such as basil, thyme and oregano

Cook the rice according to the packet instructions and drain when cooked. Preheat the oven to 180°C. Line a baking tray with baking paper.

While the rice is cooking, cut the tops off the tomatoes and courgettes and use a spoon to hollow out the insides. Place the tops and the lower parts on the lined baking tray. Cut the peppers in half and remove and discard their cores. Add to the baking tray and drizzle with 2 tablespoons of the oil and season with salt.

Heat the rest of the oil in a large pan over a medium heat and fry the onion and mushrooms for 10 minutes. Add the cooked and drained rice, the cherry tomatoes, olives, capers and raisins, if using, and cook for a further 2 minutes. Add the herbs and check the seasoning. Spoon the filling into the vegetables. Cook for 30 minutes or until the vegetables are slightly soft. To serve, place the hats back on the courgettes and tomatoes.

Les petites astuces – tips *If you can't find round courgettes, use 2 very large courgettes, halved lengthways, with the seeds scraped out.

You can use leftover roast meat in place of the mushrooms, if you prefer.

Faire en avance – get ahead The stuffing can be made a couple of days in advance.

Farçous aux blettes et citron confit

CHARD AND PRESERVED LEMON BLINIS

Although originally from Aveyron, I first spotted a *farçou* at the market in Montpellier, cooked by a little lady on her stall, to be eaten on the go. It is a pancake packed with chard, and quite unlike your average French market fare, which usually consists of large vats of choucroute garnie, paellas or rotisserie chickens. Only an hour after my first *farçou* experience I was enjoying a gastro version in a smart local restaurant, Le Pastis, cooked by an ex-Paris-based chef Daniel Lutrand, who champions the local produce. He served a delicate, light version as an *amuse bouche*. Inspired by the preserved lemons that are popular in Provence, I've studded mine with little citrus hits; a lovely match with wholesome chard.

Makes 8 large or 16 small
Preparation time: 5 minutes
Cooking time: 15 minutes

150g plain white flour

1 tsp baking powder

a pinch of salt

1 shallot, peeled and finely chopped

1 clove of garlic, peeled and
finely minced

½ tbsp preserved lemon,
finely chopped

3 chard leaves, finely chopped

200ml milk

2 eggs, beaten

2 tbsp butter

optional: 4 tbsp crème fraîche

Mix together the flour, baking powder and salt. Add the shallot, garlic, lemon and chard. Mix together, and then stir in the milk and eggs.

Heat the butter in a large non-stick frying pan over a medium heat. When the butter melts, use a spoon or small ladle to drop some of the batter into the pan and quickly flatten it down. Fry in batches so as not to overcrowd the pan. Fry for 3–4 minutes on one side or until golden brown before flipping and cooking on the other side for a further 3–4 minutes. Serve warm with a dollop of crème fraîche. They can also be enjoyed cold.

Une petite astuce – tip The chard can be replaced with 50g of baby spinach or kale, finely chopped.

Faire en avance – get ahead These can be made a few hours ahead and reheated in the oven at 160°C for 15 minutes. You can also make the batter in advance and keep it covered in cling film in the fridge for a couple of days.

Daube Provençale au rosé

PROVENÇAL VEAL ROSÉ STEW

The French love a good stew so it didn't surprise me to spot a *daube* on menus – and even in jars at the supermarket – in Provence. There's not much that makes their version stand out from its regional cousins: cheap cuts of beef, a bottle of red wine, some vegetables and herbs. It does, however, have its own special pot, a *daubière*, which is made from clay and doesn't allow any steam to escape, keeping all the flavour trapped inside. I'm not sure whether a special pot will make a stew taste that much better, but the choice of ingredients, plus the magic of slow cooking certainly will. A pink blushing rosé, green olives, saffron and fennel replace the classic *daube* ingredients in my recipe – some of the flavours of Provence that I enjoyed most.

Serves 4–6
Preparation time: 20 minutes
Cooking time: 2¾ hours

1.5kg veal shoulder, cut into large chunks

2 tbsp plain white flour

2 tbsp vegetable oil

2 onions, peeled and quartered

3 cloves of garlic, peeled and crushed

4 carrots, peeled

1 head of fennel, chopped (reserve the green sprigs for a garnish)

500ml rosé wine

750ml water

2 pinches of saffron

10 black peppercorns

2 bay leaves

3 sprigs of fresh thyme

20 green olives

sea salt, to taste

Dust the veal in the flour. Heat the oil in a large pot over a medium to high heat and fry the meat until golden on all sides (don't overcrowd the pan; you may need to fry it in batches).

Remove the veal, add the onions and garlic and fry for a couple of minutes until the garlic is soft. Add all the other ingredients and return the veal to the pot. Cover with a lid and leave to simmer very gently for 2½ hours or until the meat is almost falling apart.

To serve, remove all the vegetables and meat and set aside. Pour everything else through a fine sieve and then return the vegetables and meat to the pan with the stock.

Sprinkle over the reserved green fennel sprigs and serve with a big bowl of pasta (such as tagliatelle) tossed in a little olive oil or some jacket potatoes.

Les petites astuces – tips The veal can be replaced with beef for a heartier dish or chicken for a more delicate flavour. Use a whole chicken that has been jointed and cook for about an hour (or until the meat starts to fall off the bone). The beef may need a little longer than the veal.

Faire en avance – get ahead Like all stews, it will taste even better if you make it the day before and allow time for the flavours to develop. Gently reheat for 45 minutes in an oven preheated to 160°C, stirring occasionally.

Joues de lotte de mer en croûte de noisette avec une salade

HAZELNUT-CRUSTED MONKFISH CHEEKS WITH A SUNSHINE SALAD

At the old port in Marseille you can find the local fisherman selling their catch – unless the waters have been rough the night before, in which case only the bravest fisherman will venture out. Among the sardines, red mullet, sea bass and John Dory, you'll also find monkfish. These fish are truly quite ugly and certainly look like they live on the bottom of the sea but, despite their scary appearance, I love them for their firm texture and almost boneless meat. Most people eat the tail, which is the meatiest part of the fish, but I'm a firm believer in 'nose-to-tail' eating and monkfish cheeks are lovely little bone-free nuggets of flesh. Like the tail, they have a substantial meaty texture which pairs excellently with this crunchy nutty crust. Serve with a bright plate of sunshine salad made from carrot, grapefruit and radish.

Serves 4

Preparation time: 20 minutes
Cooking time: 10 minutes

50g white breadcrumbs

150g hazelnuts, finely chopped

8 monkfish cheeks

salt and freshly ground pepper

zest of 1 grapefruit (use the fruit, segmented, in the salad)

50g melted butter

a drizzle of olive oil

For the salad

10 radishes, finely sliced

½ a watermelon radish, finely sliced (or replace with another 10 normal radishes)

1 carrot, peeled into ribbons with a speed peeler

2–3 tbsp extra virgin olive oil

Toast the breadcrumbs and hazelnuts in a dry non-stick pan until golden. Season the monkfish all over with salt and pepper. Mix together the toasted breadcrumbs and hazelnuts with the grapefruit zest and melted butter.

Heat a large frying pan with the oil until smoking hot. Place the monkfish cheeks in the pan and turn the heat down to medium. Fry for 3 minutes or until the underside is golden, and then turn over and cook for another 3 minutes. Transfer the cooked cheeks to a plate and top with the crunchy topping.

Toss the radishes, grapefruit segments and carrot with the oil. Season, to taste, with salt and pepper. Serve immediately with the monkfish cheeks.

Les petites astuces – tips Don't dress your salad too far in advance. The salt will draw water from the radishes and make the salad watery and soggy.

If you can't find monkfish cheeks, you can replace with cod cheeks, allowing four per person. Alternatively, monkfish tail cut into 2cm-thick slices works too.

Nathalie   Rachel   Pierre   Lorena

Adrien   *Antonin*   *Aurelien*   *Julie*

Ratatouille en escabeche

APERITIF RATATOUILLE

In Paris, the first signs of sunshine at the end of the winter come via the markets. Even if it's still grey and cold, the brightly coloured produce from the South of France starts to appear. The pungent new-season garlic with its slightly violet waxy skin, the bulging fat globe artichokes, the deep purple aubergines . . . the colours explode when the weather gets hotter and it's difficult to resist the rainbow array of vegetables. These vegetables are ideal served as an aperitif with some cheese and charcuterie, tossed with pasta, or on top of a pizza.

Makes a 1 litre jar *Preparation time: 40 minutes • Cooking time: 15–20 minutes • Marinating time: 3 days*

1 red pepper • 1 yellow pepper • 1 courgette, sliced lengthways into 3mm-thick slices • 1 aubergine, sliced lengthways into 3mm-thick slices • 225ml extra virgin olive oil • zest and juice of 1 lemon (keep the lemon halves) • 2 globe artichokes • 1.5 litres water • 325ml white wine vinegar • salt • 2 bulbs of garlic, cloves separated and peeled • 2 tsp dried oregano • a pinch of sugar • 6 fresh basil leaves

Arrange the peppers on a baking tray lined with baking paper and place under a hot grill. Turn every so often until they blacken all over, then put them in a freezer bag and seal tightly. Once cool, remove the skin and tear the flesh into large strips, discarding the seeds and core. Heat a griddle pan until very hot. Toss the courgette and aubergine slices in oil until they are coated. Arrange the slices on the griddle pan (don't crowd the pan; cook them in batches) and cook for 3 minutes or until they have brown griddle marks. Turn the vegetables over and cook on the other side. Set aside until needed.

Have lemon halves and a bowl of water mixed with the lemon juice at the ready. Trim the tips off the first artichoke, about 5cm down the leaves, and trim the stalk to about 5cm. Peel away the dark outer layers of the stalk. Rub regularly with cut lemon to avoid discoloration. Peel away the toughest outer leaves, and with the help of a small sharp knife cut the darkest leaves off until you reach the paler, greenish-yellow leaves underneath. Cut the head into quarters and scoop out and discard the hairy choke with a teaspoon. Place in the bowl with water and lemon juice, while prepping the other artichoke.

Bring the 1.5 litres of water to the boil with 200ml of the vinegar and a pinch of salt. Once it has come to a boil add the artichoke quarters and the peeled garlic cloves. Cook for a further 5 minutes or until al dente. Drain and place the artichokes and garlic on a clean tea towel.

Mix together the oregano with the remaining oil and vinegar, the sugar and a pinch of salt. Half-fill the sterilized jar with layers of the vegetables, the lemon zest and basil. Top with the oil mixture, making sure there are no air bubbles (use a chopstick to release any trapped air). Repeat until everything is used up. The vegetables should be submerged in the oil; if not, top up with a little more olive oil. Seal the jar and leave for a minimum of 3 days to marinate. Keep in a cool dark space.

Ravioli Niçois grillés

PAN-FRIED NICE RAVIOLI

I lost count of the number of fresh pasta shops I spotted in Nice. The locals nip in on their way home from work to pick up a bag for dinner and more often than not they choose *Ravioli Niçois*. This ravioli is a pretty clever way of using up any leftovers from the *daube Provençale* (see page 148), as the slowly cooked meat makes a delicious filling alongside Nice's most popular vegetable, chard, and some local mature goat's cheese. In my local neighbourhood in Paris there are countless little Chinese dumpling bars. I love the contrast of textures in these dumplings: the crunchy base and the slightly chewy skin. Combining the *Niçois* filling with a crisp and chewy casing works really well, even if it's not strictly traditional.

Serves 4–6

Preparation time: 30 minutes
Resting time: 15 minutes–2 hours
Cooking time: 10 minutes
Equipment: a 5cm crimped biscuit cutter (or a glass)

For the dough

250g plain white flour, plus extra for dusting

180ml just boiled water

2 tbsp vegetable oil

150ml water

For the filling

200g leftover *daube Provencale* or Sunday roast (approx. 150g meat and 50g vegetables)

50g fresh chard or baby spinach

50g Tomme de Chèvre (rindless), mature hard goat's cheese or Parmesan cheese, finely grated

Tip the flour into a bowl and make a well in the centre. Pour in the just boiled water and stir together till you have a very crumbly, lumpy dough. Knead until it comes together into a ball. If the dough is very dry add a tablespoon of water. Transfer the dough to a flour-dusted work surface and knead for about 5 minutes until the dough is smooth and springs back when touched.

Roll the dough in a little flour and place it in a freezer bag. Seal the bag and leave it to rest at room temperature for at least 15 minutes. Prepare the filling. Finely chop the leftover *daube Provençale* and chard and mix together with the grated cheese.

Lightly dust the work surface and a large plate with flour. Divide the rested dough into quarters. Roll one quarter into a long rectangle about 5cm wide and 3mm thick. Place a heaped teaspoon of the filling 2.5cm from the end and fold the end over to cover the filling. Press down firmly, making sure to press out any air pockets. Use the biscuit cutter to cut out a half-moon shape and trim the excess pastry. Place the ravioli on the plate dusted with flour. Repeat with the rest of the dough and filling, squeezing together the leftover bits of dough and rerolling.

Heat the oil in a large non-stick pan until smoking hot, then add the ravioli in batches. Turn down the heat and cook for 2 minutes or until the base of each is golden. Add 150ml water, cover with the lid and cook for 8 minutes until the water evaporates. Serve immediately. Great with the Espelette ketchup or xipista sauce (see pages 125 or 112).

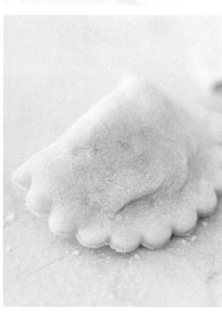

Millefeuilles au fromage de chèvre, fraises et concombre

GOAT'S CHEESE, STRAWBERRY AND CUCUMBER MILLEFEUILLES

Is this a starter, dessert or cheese course? For me, it could easily masquerade as any of the three with its salty goat's cheese, cooling and crisp cucumber and sweet, but ever so slightly acidic, Gariguette strawberries. Take your pick, as this is a refreshing dish that I think transcends any rigid mealtime conventions.

Makes 6
Preparation time: 20 minutes
Cooking time: 10 minutes

6 tbsp butter

2 tbsp runny honey

4 sheets of filo pastry (roughly 48cm x 22cm)

1 x 250g goat's cheese log, crumbled

20 basil leaves

1 large cucumber

2 tbsp white balsamic vinegar

200g ripe, firm Gariguette strawberries (or other strawberries), sliced

Preheat the oven to 160°C. Melt the butter and 1 tablespoon of the honey together in a small saucepan. Place a sheet of filo pastry on the work surface with the long side facing you. Brush the butter and honey mixture over the pastry.

Sprinkle over 100g of the cheese and then top with 10 of the basil leaves (bear in mind that the sheet will be cut into 10 rectangles, so there should be a basil leaf in each piece, so arrange the leaves in two rows of five). Place a second sheet of pastry on top and brush with the butter and honey. Cut in half lengthways and then into 10 rectangles and place on a baking sheet. Repeat with the remaining filo sheets (reserving the remaining 50g of cheese). Bake for 10 minutes or until the pastry is slightly golden.

Meanwhile, use a speed peeler to peel long cucumber ribbons (discarding the soggy centre with the seeds). Mix together the remaining honey with the balsamic vinegar and toss to coat the cucumber ribbons, strawberry slices and the remaining crumbled goat's cheese.

When ready to serve, place a pastry rectangle on each plate and top with some of the salad. Top with another pastry layer, more of the salad and a final layer of the pastry. Repeat to make the other 5 portions. You will be left with two pastry rectangles, which you can eat like crackers.

Une petite astuce – tip Replace the strawberries with tomatoes.

Petits encornets au basilic avec pois chiches à la sanguine et tomate

BASIL BABY SQUID WITH BLOOD ORANGE AND TOMATO CHICKPEAS

In the Luberon valley is a village, Rousillon, where warm tones of yellows, oranges and reds are everywhere to be seen. The colours and scenery have inspired artists for centuries, including Paul Cézanne who was born in Aix-en-Provence and who produced numerous paintings depicting the local landscape. This region was particularly well known for its ochre pigments, mined from the natural stone in the region, and all the houses in the area are painted in similar earthy tones. The local cooperative, *ôkhra*, is keeping the tradition alive with educational workshops and a shop selling the traditional ochre pigments. Spot the colours of Provence in this dish . . .

Serves 4

Preparation time: 15 minutes
Soaking time: overnight
Cooking time: 1 hour

250g dried chickpeas, rinsed

4 tbsp olive oil, plus extra to drizzle

2 cloves of garlic, peeled and finely chopped

2 large tomatoes, roughly chopped

salt and freshly ground pepper

250g baby squid, cleaned

2 blood oranges, peeled and sliced

10 basil leaves, plus a couple to garnish

Soak the chickpeas in cold water overnight. In the morning, replace the water and boil for 45 minutes. Drain and run under cold water.

Heat 2 tablespoons of the oil in a frying pan until very hot. Add the garlic, tomatoes and chickpeas. Toss and fry for 5 minutes, until the garlic is golden and the tomatoes are soft. Season with salt and pepper and tip on to a large serving plate.

Heat the rest of the oil in the pan and, when very hot, add the squid. Cook for a couple of minutes then remove from the heat and stir through the oranges and basil. Serve on top of the chickpeas and garnish with extra basil leaves and a drizzle of oil.

Une petite astuce – tip If you can't get hold of baby squid, use large squid cut into rings.

Faire en avance – get ahead The salad can be made in advance and eaten cold.

Poisson et panisse

FISH AND CHICKPEA CHIPS

The French aren't big on snacking; they are far more notorious for making an event of their main meals. In Nice, on the other hand, they have a penchant for *panisse*-nibbling between meals. A chickpea cake sliced into rounds, fingers or cubes, fried and then sprinkled with salt or dusted with icing sugar for the kids, *panisse* can also pop up as an accompaniment to main courses or as a crunchy salad garnish. I love serving them as chips alongside fried fish and a spicy harissa mayonnaise which gives a nod to Marseille's trading history with North Africa.

Serves 4
Preparation time: 30 minutes
Resting time: 15 minutes
Cooking time: 30 minutes
Equipment: a 30cm x 20cm baking dish

500g small fish (e.g. small sardines, anchovies, herring or whitebait)

100g chickpea flour

2 egg whites

1 litre vegetable oil

For the chickpea chips

500ml water

1 lemon, finely zested and cut into wedges, to serve

a pinch of salt

1 tbsp olive oil, plus extra to grease

140g chickpea flour

1 x mayonnaise recipe (see page 276)

optional: 1 heaped tsp harissa paste

Pour the water into a large pot and add half the lemon zest, the salt and the oil. Bring to a simmer over a medium heat, and then pour in the flour. Stir with a wooden spoon or heatproof spatula while the mixture thickens. Stir for a good 5 minutes.

Grease the baking dish with oil and then pour in the mixture. Spread it out to 1cm thick and then leave to cool in the fridge. Meanwhile, make the mayonnaise (see page 276), stirring in the harissa paste at the end, if using.

Preheat the oven to 100°C. Pat the fish dry. Place three plates in front of you; spread the flour on one, the egg whites on another and leave the third empty. Dip the fish first in the flour, then in the egg whites and then again in the flour. Shake off any excess flour and place on the clean plate.

Pour the oil into a heavy-based pan to a depth of at least 3cm, and place over a high heat. You can check the oil is hot enough by dropping in a small piece of bread; it should fry and sizzle as soon as it hits the oil. Gently place a few of the fish in the hot oil (do not crowd the pan). Fry for 2 minutes on one side before turning over and frying for 2 minutes on the other side, or until golden brown all over. Transfer to a wire rack and keep in the warm oven while you cook the rest.

Unmold the chickpea mixture carefully and slice it into 1cm-thick chips. Be careful, as it will break easily. Fry batches until golden brown on all sides, keeping the cooked ones warm on the wire rack in the oven. Sprinkle with salt and serve immediately with the fish and mayonnaise.

Socca avec anchoïade

CHICKPEA PANCAKES WITH ANCHOVY SPREAD

Socca is Nice's answer to the Breton *galette* (see page 18) with the southern ingredient, chickpea flour, replacing the northern buckwheat flour. I ate mine red-hot with a generous dusting of black pepper in Menton (a town just near the Italian border), which is *the* way to eat it (although you can sometimes spot the odd café serving it topped with salad and cheese like a *crêpe*). Cooked in a searing hot oven, the best *socca* are super-crunchy and charred from the heat. Unfortunately, the little oven in my Paris kitchen just doesn't get hot enough so I get my frying pan as hot as I can to recreate a similar effect.

Makes 8–10 pancakes
Preparation time: 10 minutes
Cooking time: 20 minutes

800ml water

320g chickpea flour

a pinch of salt

4 tbsp olive oil

1 small red onion, peeled and finely sliced

For the anchovy spread

250g tinned anchovies, drained

2 cloves of garlic, peeled

zest and juice of ½ a lemon

100ml extra virgin olive oil

freshly ground pepper

Whisk the water into the chickpea flour with the salt until you have a smooth paste. Chill in the fridge while preparing the anchovy spread.

Use a pestle and mortar to crush the anchovies, garlic and lemon zest to a fine paste. Mix in the oil and lemon juice. (Alternatively, you can use a blender, which will make for a smoother paste). Add pepper, to taste.

Use some kitchen towel to grease a large non-stick frying pan with a little oil then heat until very hot. Whisk the batter to make sure the flour hasn't sunk to the bottom. Pour a ladleful of the batter into the pan and swirl it around (like you would when making a *crêpe*) and sprinkle with some sliced onion. Cook for a couple of minutes until golden before flipping and cooking on the other side. Repeat until all the batter is used, greasing the pan with more oil before cooking each pancake. Keep the pancakes warm in a low oven while you cook the rest.

Spread with some of the anchovy paste and roll up or cut like a pizza. Serve immediately.

Une petite astuce – tip Use good-quality anchovies preserved in olive oil. If the ones you buy are very salty, rinse them carefully and dry them with kitchen towel.

Faire en avance – get ahead The chickpea batter will keep in the fridge for a couple of days. The anchovy spread will also keep for three or four days.

Tian Provençal

PROVENÇAL VEGETABLE BAKE

If you have seen the animated film *Ratatouille* you will know that Rémy, the rat, shows the kitchen porter how to make a ratatouille. Real ratatouille connoisseurs, however, will have immediately recognized that it is actually not a ratatouille at all, but a typical *tian*. Both ratatouille and *tian* use the same vegetables, but the main difference is in the cooking technique. A 'real' ratatouille requires cooking the vegetables individually, before bringing all the elements together at the end; a *tian* is an artful arrangement of vegetable slices, which is baked like a gratin. It's a simplified, but more often than not, better looking version of a ratatouille. And a *tian* is also the large earthenware cooking pot traditionally used in Provence.

Serves 4–6

Preparation time: 30 minutes
Cooking time: 40–45 minutes
Equipment: a 19cm round ovenproof dish

4 red onions, peeled and finely sliced

4 cloves of garlic, peeled and crushed

4 sprigs of fresh thyme

4 tbsp olive oil

1 aubergine (approx. 250g)

1 courgette (approx. 160g)

5 firm tomatoes (plum tomatoes work well)

a pinch of salt

Preheat the oven to 180°C. Fry the onions, garlic and thyme in 2 tablespoons of the oil for about 10 minutes, until soft and starting to turn golden.

Meanwhile very finely slice the aubergine and courgette crossways (2mm thick). Use a mandolin or the slicer on the side of a box grater if you have one. Slice the tomatoes into 3mm-thick slices.

Tip the softened onions, garlic and thyme into the ovenproof dish and top with a few slices of the vegetables to make a flat surface. Arrange the rest of the sliced vegetables, alternating the colours, in a circular arrangement around the dish. Drizzle with the rest of the oil and sprinkle with salt. Cook in the oven for 35–40 minutes or until the vegetables are soft and golden on top.

Une petite astuce – tip I like to eat this with cheese on toast or a baked potato.

Faire en avance – get ahead This can be made a day in advance and eaten at room temperature or reheated in the oven at 160°C for 20–30 minutes.

Truffes aux chataignes et chocolat

CHOCOLATE CHESTNUT TRUFFLES

Provence celebrates the chestnut in all its glory, particularly during its peak season of late autumn, when village fêtes, featuring *degustations* of roasted chestnuts and musical entertainment come to town. Living in France has certainly fuelled my love of chestnuts, whether simply roasted, or in the form of *crème de marron*, the sweet purée featured in the Mont Blanc dessert. This little recipe is utterly addictive, perfect with a strong cup of coffee or for edible Christmas gifts. Try these once and you'll be finding any excuse to make them again.

Makes 18–20 truffles

Preparation time: 10 minutes
Resting time: 30 minutes
Cooking time: 10 minutes
Equipment: a digital thermometer

335g dark chocolate

200g cooked chestnuts

50g butter, softened

50g sugar

2 tsp vanilla extract

Place 85g of chocolate in a heatproof bowl over a pan of simmering water (make sure the bowl doesn't touch the hot water). Melt the chocolate and then remove from the heat and leave to cool a little. In the meantime, blend all the other ingredients in a food processor.

Combine the melted chocolate with the chestnut mixture and mix well. Roll into walnut-sized balls and then refrigerate for 30 minutes. If the mixture becomes too soft to shape, chill for a few minutes in the fridge.

To coat the truffles start by tempering the chocolate.* Melt the remaining 250g chocolate over a pan of simmering water, as before. You want it to reach 45°C on a thermometer. Then you need to cool the chocolate to 27°C. You can do this by placing the bowl over another bowl of icy water and stirring it until the temperature drops. The cooled chocolate must then be reheated to 31°C, and then it is ready to use

Dip the truffles in the chocolate (a fork is useful here) and place them on a wire rack to set. Store in an airtight container in the fridge (although they are better eaten at room temperature, like all chocolate).

Les petites astuces – tips *Tempering chocolate gives it a lovely shiny finish and satisfying snap when you bite into it. You can temper chocolate in a microwave but check it every 10 seconds or so with a thermometer so it doesn't overheat. When the chocolate has almost completely melted, remove it from the microwave and stir until smooth. It should have thickened slightly.

Faire en avance – get ahead These keep well in the fridge for up to a fortnight.

Tartelette Tropézienne

TROPEZ TARTLET

The *Tarte Tropézienne's* reputation precedes it. Before I had ever seen or eaten one, the more I heard about this St Tropez specialty, the more I started imagining something exotic with rum and tropical fruits. When I finally had one in Nice, I was slightly taken aback by its simplicity; it was a basic flat brioche cake filled with pastry cream. It was delicious nevertheless. But if I had invented the *Tarte Tropézienne*, this is how I would have made it.

Makes 8

Preparation time: 30 minutes
Cooking time: 1½ hours
Equipment: an 8cm round biscuit cutter

½ a large ripe pineapple, peeled and cut into 2mm slices

100g icing sugar, sifted

8 thick slices of good-quality brioche (see page 218)

1–2 heaped tbsp very soft butter

For the pastry cream

3 egg yolks

40g sugar

20g cornflour

250ml whole milk

½ vanilla pod

optional: 1 tbsp rum

Preheat the oven to 100°C. Line a baking tray with baking paper. Pat the pineapple slices dry with kitchen towel and then dip them in the icing sugar, making sure the whole surface of each slice is covered. Place on the lined baking tray, not touching, and bake for 1½ hours.

Remove the slices from the baking paper as soon as they come out of the oven, otherwise they will stick to it. Leave to cool on a wire rack. Meanwhile, make the pastry cream. Whisk the egg yolks with the sugar until pale and thick, then whisk in the cornflour until a trail is left behind on the surface when the whisk is lifted. Pour the milk into a small saucepan. Split the vanilla pod in half lengthwise and scrape out the seeds. Add the vanilla pod and seeds to the milk, bring to the boil and then remove from the heat. Discard the vanilla pod and pour the hot milk in a slow stream over the egg mixture, whisking vigorously all the time.

Return the mixture to a clean pan and continuously whisk over a medium heat. Make sure to scrape the sides and the bottom, or it will burn. The cream will start to thicken. Once it releases a bubble or two, take it off the heat and stir in the rum (if using). Pour the mixture into a piping bag or freezer bag with the corner snipped off and refrigerate for at least an hour before using.

Cut out 8 rounds from the brioche using the biscuit cutter. Butter both sides, then place the slices in a non-stick pan. Fry gently for a couple of minutes on each side or until golden. Pipe a thick layer of pastry cream on to each slice of brioche. Top with several slices of pineapple and serve immediately.

Syllabub au rosé et aux fraises Gariguette

ROSÉ AND STRAWBERRY SYLLABUB

If you have a soft spot for strawberries and cream (and what self-respecting Brit doesn't?), you'll love this poshed-up version of the summertime classic. The South of France is blessed with sun-kissed strawberries, equal to our luscious British ones, and they are an irresistible match for another fixture in the south: rosé wine. Fold the rosé syrup into a puffy cloud of Chantilly cream and you have a perfect *al fresco* dessert in a dash.

Serves 4–6
Preparation time: 15 minutes
Cooking time: 5 minutes

175ml rosé wine

80g sugar

½ tsp rose water

200ml whipping cream

a pinch of salt

250g strawberries, halved
or quartered if large

Bring the wine and sugar to the boil in a small saucepan. Whisk until the sugar has dissolved then remove from the heat and leave to cool completely before adding the rose water.

In a bowl, whip the cream with a pinch of salt to stiff peaks.* Fold in the cool rosé syrup and half the strawberries. Serve immediately with the rest of the strawberries on top.

Les petites astuces – tips For a non-alcoholic version replace the rosé with a clear apple juice.

*Make sure the cream is extra cold and use a metal bowl that has been in the freezer for 30 minutes; this will make whipping the cream easier.

Faire en avance – get ahead The rosé sugar syrup can be made in advance and kept in the fridge until needed.

ARTICHAUT "VIOLET de PROVENCE"

A visit to a Provençal wild flower and herb garden.

Le jardin de nos grands-mères

OUVERT UNIQUEMENT LE SAMEDI

Charlotte aux herbes et fleurs de Provence

MELON CHARLOTTE WITH CRYSTALLIZED FLOWERS

I'm partial to a retro dessert and you don't get much more retro than a ribbon-bound Charlotte. I remember making my first *Charlotte aux fraises* (strawberry Charlotte) when I was studying *patisserie*. It was a rather fiddly job, and the lengthy process began with piping our own sponge fingers before trimming them to equal size to fit the cake tin. I've decided to take a shortcut and use shop-bought ones here. A ripe, perfumed cantaloupe melon is a great match for summery-scented basil, one of the quintessential herbs of Provence.

Serves 8–10

Preparation time: 30 minutes

Resting time: overnight

Chilling time: 2 hours

Equipment: a 20–22cm cake ring, or a springform cake tin with the base removed; a paintbrush; 40cm ribbon

18g leaf gelatin

500g ripe cantaloupe melon flesh

4 large basil leaves

30 sponge fingers

400ml whipping cream

80g sugar

200g fromage frais

For the crystallized flowers

2 good handfuls of edible flowers (pansies, violets, nasturtiums, rose petals) and basil leaves

1 egg white, lightly whisked

3 tbsp sugar

Line a baking tray with baking paper. Line a baking tray with baking paper. Trim the flowers, removing the stem and the sepals. Set aside one handful of the flowers and leave unfrosted. Using the paintbrush, brush each flower lightly with egg white, then sprinkle with sugar, holding the flower by the back of its head, or as delicately as possible if using rose petals. Shake gently to remove any excess sugar and place each one on the lined baking tray. Coat the basil leaves in the same way. Leave to rest in a cool dark place overnight until crisp to the touch.

Soak the gelatin in a large bowl of cold water. Blend half the melon with the 4 large basil leaves until smooth. Pour into a saucepan, bring to the boil and then remove from the heat and leave to cool to room temperature. Squeeze the water from the gelatin and stir it into the cooled melon mixture until dissolved. Chill in the fridge.

Place the cake ring on your serving plate. If the sponge fingers have rounded ends, cut one end so they are straight. Line the fingers around the inside of the cake tin, making sure they sit tightly together (straight edge on the plate). If they start to fall into the tin, a second pair of hands may be required.

Whip the cream with the sugar until it forms stiff peaks. Chop the rest of the melon into small cubes. Beat the fromage frais into the cold blended melon and then fold into the cream with the cubes of melon. Pour into the cake ring and chill in the fridge for 2 hours.

To serve, remove the ring and tie the ribbon around the cake. Decorate with the crystallized and reserved flowers and basil.

Bavarois au fromage blanc et rhubarb avec une tuile

BOAT BAVAROIS WITH ORANGE BLOSSOM BISCUIT SAIL

Navette is not only 'boat' in French, but also the name of a very popular biscuit in the South of France. Most often perfumed with orange flower water, these biscuits are somewhat hard and dry, and are, as far as I'm concerned, an acquired taste. So I decided to make my own boat scene: a fromage blanc *bavarois* boat floating in a sea of cool pink rhubarb with a biscuit sail. Now this is the kind of *navette* that floats my boat.

Makes 6
Preparation time: 30 minutes
Resting time: at least 2 hours
Cooking time: 10 minutes
Equipment: 6 x 90ml ramekins or moulds

500g pink rhubarb, cut into 5cm pieces

200g sugar

For the bavarois

4g leaf gelatin, soaked for 10 minutes in cold water

40g sugar

2 egg whites

200g fromage blanc

½ tsp vanilla extract

For the biscuit sail

25ml orange juice

60g sugar

1 tsp orange flower water

1 heaped tbsp plain white flour

30g butter, melted and cooled

Put the 40g of sugar and several tablespoons of water in a saucepan and bring to the boil for 2 minutes. Make sure the sugar dissolves, then remove from the heat. Wait for the bubbles to stop rising and then whisk the gelatin into the sugar syrup.

Whisk the egg whites until foamy and white then very gradually pour the sugar syrup over them. Continue to whisk until soft peaks form. Beat the fromage blanc and the vanilla extract together and then whisk into the egg white mixture until just incorporated. Divide between the individual ramekins and leave in the fridge to set for at least 2 hours.

Pour 200ml of water into a saucepan and add the rhubarb and the 200g of sugar. Bring to the boil for 2 minutes before removing from the heat. Leave to cool a little before chilling in the fridge. Ten minutes before serving, place the rhubarb in the freezer.

Preheat the oven to 180°C. Line a baking tray with waxed baking paper or a silicon mat. To make the sail, whisk together the orange juice, sugar and orange flower water. Sift in the flour while continuously whisking and add the butter. Pour a ladleful of the batter into the middle of the lined tray and spread the batter evenly with an angled spatula, to a rectangle 12cm wide and 2mm thick (the length isn't as important). Cook in the oven for 8–10 minutes, then leave to rest for a minute before cutting into triangles. Unmould the bavarois into serving dishes. Pour over the ice cold rhubarb syrup and scatter around some rhubarb pieces. Place a 'sail' on top of the bavarois and serve immediately.

Mousse au nougat

NOUGAT MOUSSE

Despite being a mainstay in the gift shops of Provence, nougat was a Middle-Eastern invention. When it began being imported to the port of Marseilles in the seventeenth century, it quickly gained favour and Gallic production began. Olivier de Serres planted almond trees in nearby Montélimar, and soon the town became synonymous with the snow-white confectionary.

The key to good nougat is choosing your honey well. Provence is known for its lavender honey, which has a subtle flavour well suited to nougat. If you can't find lavender honey, another mild honey will work. I love the taste of nougat but making it into a mousse is even easier than making the nougat itself as no sugar thermometer is needed. In its mousse guise, you'll discover a light and airy alternative to its chewy, and sometimes rock-hard, cousin, but with all those nougaty flavours.

Serves 4–6
Preparation time: 15 minutes
Resting time: 1 hour
Cooking time: 5 minutes

25g shelled pistachios, roughly chopped

50g blanched almonds, roughly chopped

100g lavender honey or other mild honey

2 tbsp water

2 small egg whites

200g whipped cream

50g candied orange peel, finely chopped

Toast the pistachios and almonds in a dry pan until golden. Place the honey and water in a saucepan over a high heat and cook for about 5 minutes. It will start to foam like crazy and then calm down.

In the meantime, whisk the eggs whites using a freestanding or handheld electric mixer until frothy. Once the honey is bubbling gently, slowly pour it over the egg whites while whisking. Continue to whisk for about 5 minutes, until the egg whites form soft peaks and are cooling slowly. Leave to cool for a few minutes. Set aside a couple of tablespoons of the pistachios, almonds and candied orange to sprinkle on top of the finished mousse then fold the rest into the egg whites with the cream.

Divide the mixture between glasses or bowls and leave to chill for at least an hour before serving. Sprinkle the reserved pistachios, almonds and candied orange on top.

---

*Une petite astuce – **tip*** This dessert can be frozen into a semifreddo. Pour the mixture into a loaf tin lined with cling film and freeze. Serve in slices.

Lyon

LE SAINT MARCELLIN

LE PÂTÉ EN CROÛTE

LA NEIGE

LE BEAUFORT

LES SAUCISSONS DE LYON

LA PRALINE

LA NOIX DE GRENOBLE

LE REBLOCHON

LES COUSSINS DE LYON

LE BROCHET

LES QUENELLES

LE BOUCHON

LE CHALET

LA MONTAGNE

LA TOQUE

LA FONDUE

SUISSE

ITALIE

LYON

SAINT ETIENNE

ANNECY

CHAMONIX MONT BLANC

LES ALPES

GRENOBLE

VALENCE

RHÔNE

THE ALMIGHTY FRENCH LION, SWEET MEATS AND SNOWY PEAKS

Lyon is the capital of French gastronomy, the home of the godfather of modern French cuisine, Paul Bocuse, and has easy access to Burgundy and the Côtes du Rhône appellations. It all sounds rather grand, but actually Lyon's reputation for good food comes from humble roots.

After the French Revolution of the nineteenth century, a number of women, many of them previously cooks for *bourgeois* families in Lyon, started serving meals to the *canuts* (the workers from the silk factories). *Les mères Lyonnaises*, as they became called, began opening eateries serving simple home-cooked fare that was impeccably prepared. It wasn't just the silk workers who came to eat their food; its quality and affordability attracted people from all different backgrounds. Some of the eateries gained reputations as great as any Paris restaurant at the time: Eugènie Brazier went so far as to be awarded 3 Michelin stars in 1933 – the first woman to receive such an honour and no small feat for any chef.

With all this in the back of my mind, Lyon had a great gastronomic reputation to live up to. My first port of call was, of course, lunch at a *bouchon*, the traditional Lyonnais eatery. My first *bouchon* experience was no light matter, not only because I had high hopes but also because I experienced, firsthand, the Lyonnais love of nose-to-tail eating and super-sized portions. The meal kicked off with a lovely green salad with delicate lamb sweetbreads and an excellent dressing. It was followed by a classic Lyonnais plate of chicken liver pudding with tomato coulis and dumplings. Now, one would think that this would be enough, but accompaniments came fast and furiously from the kitchen: a side of potato gratin, seasonal vegetables, macaroni cheese and a loaded bread basket. I barely managed to make a dent. Even though I was almost bursting at the seams, I couldn't resist going for one of my favourite French desserts: *île flottante*, a poached meringue in a pool of light custard. This one boasted a pink praline centre, adding a delicious crunch to the dish from the caramelized almonds. Needless to say I rolled out of the *bouchon*.

My next stop was Les Halles de Lyon Paul Bocuse – a food hall filled with specialties from the Lyon region and further field. Sausages were strung up from the ceiling at the butcher's counter, large pink-stained brioches were temptingly piled up, oozy Saint-Marcellin cheese enticed at La Mere Richard cheese stand (the cheesemonger will ask when you want to eat the cheese and will select accordingly) and cylindrical *quenelles*, the artisan Lyonnais dumplings, were neatly lined up everywhere. It was the ideal homage to Paul Bocuse, who invented the concept of *nouvelle cuisine*, a food movement that aimed to showcase quality ingredients and offer a lighter and less opulent approach to dining.

Eating in Lyon certainly felt like a sporting event and my stomach was stretched into new dimensions. Luckily the French Alps are only an hour away, providing the perfect place to work off those extra pounds and build up a new appetite from skiing and hiking. It's not about Michelin-starred restaurants on the slopes, of course, but wooden chalets, roaring fires, scoops of hearty *tartiflette* (cheesy bacon and potato bake) and warming onion soup.

On my first night in the sleepy little mountain village of Peisey-Nancroix, Madame Chenal, the owner of the bed and breakfast I was staying at, served cheese fondue, the mountain classic, for dinner. Madame Chenal was quite the cook, making everything from scratch, from yoghurts using milk from the local farm, through to homemade charcuterie, jams, cakes and bread. Before transport became so accessible, this style of home production was fairly common in the more remote mountain villages; people had to be a lot more self-sufficient in their approach to eating and Madame Chenal still embraces this ethos.

During my stay I discovered other lesser known, but equally enticing, dishes and ingredients: little diamond-shaped buckwheat pasta shapes called *crozet* (see page 204), mainly served as a gooey, cheesy gratin, a creamy smooth chestnut pumpkin soup and an utterly moreish walnut and caramel tart (see page 223). And, as I happened to be staying over the Easter weekend, I also discovered the cutest chocolate rabbits hiding in my room!

Simplicity is key to the cuisine of this area, and, most of the time, a good mature mountain cheese like Beaufort or Reblochon was enough to keep me happy. But despite all the skiing I did during the day I certainly didn't feel like I was going hungry at night.

Both Lyon and the bordering French Alps have wholesome home-cooked dishes at their heart which, for me, is more inspiring than any fine-dining culture. As an offal lover, Lyonnaise attitudes to making use of every part of the animal suited me to a tee and inspired a couple of dishes in this chapter.

Quenelles à la semoule

SAVOURY SEMOLINA DUMPLINGS

Lyon is the capital of *quenelles*, or, as we have less graciously named them, 'dumplings'. The most famous of them all is the *quenelle de brochet* which is made of pike. Testament to the city's obsession is the *Bar à Quenelles*, where you can grab a quick *quenelle*-on-the-go. They have many types, cooked in a variety of ways: pan-fried, steamed or in a soup. I find the simplest way is like the Italians cook their gnocchi: in boiling, salted water. There's really not much effort required when making *quenelles*, and most of the ingredients are store-cupboard staples, making them the perfect dish to whip up in less than 30 minutes.

Makes approx. 48 mini quenelles
Serves 4
Preparation time: 10 minutes
Cooking time: 5 minutes

240ml milk

40g butter

salt and freshly ground pepper

a generous pinch of freshly grated nutmeg

140g semolina flour, plus extra to dust

2 egg yolks

extra virgin olive oil, to drizzle

optional: grated strongly flavoured cheese, to serve

Flavour ideas

140g cooked spinach (drained weight), blended to a smooth paste

50g strongly flavoured cheese, grated

2–3 heaped tsp sun-dried tomato paste

Put the milk, butter, a pinch of salt and pepper and the nutmeg in a pan and bring to the boil. Remove from the heat and, using a wooden spoon, beat in the semolina with the egg yolks. At this point, beat in one of the flavourings, if using. Make sure to beat hard and fast, otherwise the semolina will become lumpy, until it comes together into a smooth dough.

Dust a plate or baking tray with semolina. Use two teaspoons to form the dough into a quenelle shape and rest it on the plate while you finish forming the others.

Bring a large saucepan of water with a generous pinch of salt to a boil. Add all the dumplings and as soon as they rise to the top, use a slotted spoon to remove them from the water. Drain well and serve drizzled with a little oil and a sprinkling of cheese if you like.

Une petite astuce – tip Dip the teaspoons in warm water between each scoop; this will help stop the mixture sticking.

Faire en avance – get ahead Dust some cling film with semolina flour and roll the dumpling dough into a long snaky length about 2cm in diameter. Cut into 2cm pieces and freeze. The quenelle dough can also be frozen after it has been shaped.

Pâté en croûte aux pistaches et abricots

PISTACHIO, APRICOT AND PORK PIE

In search of the perfect *pâté en croûte*, I had no reluctance in trying many! Across Lyon, the delis, butchers and restaurants all claim to have designed the best, and this recipe brings together all my favourite elements for an ultimate version. This is an easy version, which leaves out the jelly to speed things up a touch.

Makes 1 loaf

Preparation time: 40 minutes
Resting time: 1 hour, or overnight
Cooking time: 2 hours
Equipment: a 900g loaf tin lined with baking paper

325g lean pork mince

325g veal or pork escalope, chopped finely but not minced

100g ready-to-eat dried apricots or soft prunes, chopped into 5mm cubes

50g shelled pistachios, roughly chopped

zest of ½ an orange

¼ tsp salt

½ tsp freshly ground pepper

a generous pinch of freshly grated nutmeg

1 egg yolk mixed with 2 tbsp milk

For the pastry

75g butter

125g lard

50ml milk

75ml hot water

a pinch of salt

375g plain white flour, plus extra for dusting

Mix together the meat, apricots, pistachios, orange zest, salt, pepper and nutmeg. Cover the bowl with cling film and leave in the fridge for at least an hour, and preferably overnight.

Place the butter, lard, milk, water and salt in a saucepan over a medium heat. Cook until all the fats have melted then remove from the heat and leave to cool slightly. Tip the flour into a bowl and make a well in the middle. Pour in the melted fats and stir together. Use your hands to shape the dough into a ball.

On a floured surface, roll out two-thirds of the dough to a rectangle 20cm x 25cm and about 5mm thick. Line the prepared tin with the dough, carefully pressing it into the corners and sides. Make sure there are no holes or cracks; fill them in with leftover pastry. Trim the excess pastry around the edges. Add the filling and flatten it so it has a level surface and there are no gaps. Preheat the oven to 180°C.

Roll out the remainder of the pastry to a rectangle a little bigger than the top of the tin. Place the pastry on top of the filling and use a fork to press down and seal the edges. Cut three little holes in the top of the pastry and brush with egg wash.

Take a piece of foil, 4cm x 4cm, and wrap it around the handle of a wooden spoon to make a tube. Insert the tube into one of the holes, then repeat with the other holes. Cut a piece of foil the size of the top of your pie with a slit in the middle. Cover the pie loosely, making sure that the vents stick out but the rest of the pastry is covered. Bake for 1½ hours, then remove the foil and bake for a further 30 minutes until crisp and brown. Remove from the oven and leave to cool before taking it out of the tin.

La nouvelle salade Lyonnaise

THE NEW LYONNAIS SALAD

After a couple of days in Lyon I was looking for something a little lighter with less of a meat bias. I came across Brazier Wine Bar, which has a fresh approach to French food, focusing more on using local seasonal produce than the classic dishes of Lyon. The menu was fairly short with only a couple of choices per course. A starter salad of smoked haddock and poached egg immediately caught my eye and was my inspiration for this main-course version which features a few of my own additions.

Serves 4

Preparation time: 15 minutes
Cooking time: 15 minutes

4 sticks of celery, trimmed

200g celeriac, peeled and very finely sliced (use a mandolin if you have one)

1 Granny Smith apple, unpeeled, cored and cubed

400g smoked haddock

600ml milk

4 fresh bay leaves

a generous pinch of freshly grated nutmeg

½ tsp white pepper

salt

4 eggs

For the dressing

zest and juice of 1 lemon

4 tbsp extra virgin olive oil

1 tbsp white wine vinegar

2 tbsp finely chopped chives

a pinch of sugar

Whisk together the dressing ingredients. Use a speed peeler to make celery ribbons, then pat them with kitchen towel to remove the excess moisture. Toss the celeriac, apple and celery with the dressing in a serving bowl.

Place the smoked haddock in a small pan with the milk, bay leaves, nutmeg and pepper. The milk should completely cover the fish. Cover with the lid and cook on a low heat for 6 minutes, or until the fish flakes apart when tested with a fork. Remove from the heat and set aside.

Bring a large pan of salted water to the boil. Pierce the larger end of the egg with a pin and gently lower each egg into the hot water. When the water returns to a boil, reduce the heat to a simmer and begin timing. Allow 6 minutes for large eggs and 5 minutes for medium, then remove and run under cold water. Peel the eggs.

Remove the fish from the milk with a slotted spoon. Peel off the skin and use a fork to flake the flesh into the bowl with the salad. Gently mix together before dividing between serving plates and placing an egg on top. Drizzle with some of the poaching milk.

Une petite astuce – tip Slicing the celeriac on a mandolin will make a world of difference to the texture. Just be careful though and use the guard!

Pizza Lyonnaise

LYONNAIS PIZZA

As a child my Mum was always trying to find clever ways to sneak offal into the family meal. Offal was, and still is, a cheap source of iron and protein, so Mum, ever one to watch the household budget, would make good use of these unfashionable off-cuts. Lyon is famous for its use of offal so I've taken a leaf out of Mum's book and mixed it up with a hint of mince for this pizza topping, making it taste slightly milder. Lots of zingy fresh flavours such as tomatoes, capers, red onions and lemon zest vamp this up into such a treat that even my offal-loathing friends can't resist tucking in.

Makes 4

Preparation time: 30 minutes
Resting time: 30 minutes
Cooking time: 20 minutes

1 x pizza dough recipe (see page 275)

150g chicken or veal liver, kidneys or heart (or a mixture), finely chopped

50g beef mince

1 red onion, peeled and finely chopped

3 tomatoes, deseeded and finely chopped

2 cloves of garlic, peeled and crushed

2 tbsp capers, finely chopped

2 tbsp olive oil

1 tsp salt

3 sprigs of fresh thyme, leaves picked

1 tbsp finely chopped fresh rosemary

½ tsp cracked black pepper

2 tbsp finely chopped parsley

zest of 1 lemon

First make the dough (see page 275). After it has rested for 30 minutes, preheat the oven to 200°C. Line two large baking trays with baking paper. Mix all the topping ingredients together.

Divide the dough into quarters and shape each piece into a ball. Dust the work surface lightly with flour and roll out the first ball to 25cm in diameter and 2mm thick. Place on one of the trays and spread with a quarter of the topping mix. Repeat with the remaining dough balls and topping so you have two pizzas to a tray.

Cook in the oven for 20 minutes or until the bases are crisp and lightly golden. Sprinkle with parsley and lemon zest just before serving.

Une petite astuce – tip If you're finding it hard to roll out the dough then use your hands to gently stretch it out.

Faire en avance – get ahead The dough can be made up to a day in advance. Keep it refrigerated in a bowl, covered in cling film or a damp tea towel.

Petits saucissons briochés

BABY BRIOCHE HOTDOGS

There are many culinary highlights from my trip to Lyon but one of them has to be the *saucisson brioché*. The typical sausage to use is a *cervelas*, which is sometimes spiked with pistachio nuts or, on the posher end of the spectrum, stuffed with truffles AND pistachios. I tested out several sausages for this recipe, but the one that kept coming out on top was the classic hotdog sausage: the Frankfurter or, as I know it, the Wiener. Wiener sausages were often served at my Austrian Grandma's table – not the cheap kind that disguise an array of artificial nastiness, but ones using good-quality meat and with a light smoky flavour. Of course, you can use any sausage you like; the key is quality and cooking time. And no hotdog is complete without a dollop of caramelized onion or try sauerkraut for an Alsacian twist.

Makes 8

Preparation time: 30 minutes
Resting time: 45 minutes
Cooking time: 40 minutes
Equipment: a 20cm x 30cm baking tray, lined with baking paper

1 x portion brioche dough (see page 218)

optional: 3–4 tbsp mustard

1 egg yolk mixed with 2 tbsp milk

4 Wiener/Frankfurter sausages, cut in half to make 8 shorter sausages

For the caramelized onions

1 onion, peeled and finely sliced

a knob of butter

a pinch of salt

a pinch of sugar

Chill the brioche dough in the fridge while you cook the onions. Fry the onions with the butter and seasoning over a medium to high heat for about 10 minutes or until the onions are golden brown. Set aside and leave to cool.

Roll out the dough to a strip roughly 60cm long and about 5cm wider than the halved sausages.

Cut the dough into 8 equal pieces and brush the dough with mustard, if using. Then brush egg wash along the edges of each rectangle. Place half a sausage in the middle and a tablespoon of the caramelized onion along the sausage. Fold the dough over the sausage, making sure to overlap the edges and press down the ends to seal. Place the buns (seam down) on the baking tray.

Brush the buns with egg wash and leave to rise in a warm place for about 45 minutes, until risen by several centimetres and puffy.

Preheat the oven to 180°C. Brush the buns a second time with egg wash and cook in the oven for 30 minutes or until a skewer inserted into the middle comes out clean (cover the buns loosely with foil if they are browning too quickly).

Leave to cool for 5 minutes before turning out on to a wire rack. These are best eaten while still warm.

Croquettes

POTATO NUGGETS

On my travels around France I always try to meet up with the locals. So it was great finding out that an old colleague, from the days when I worked at a Parisian department store, was from Lyon. I was lucky enough to catch up with Prudence and her mum over a cup of coffee. It was interesting to hear about the differences between the food cooked at home compared with the food eaten in the typical Lyonnais *bouchons* (restaurants). Both speed and resourcefulness are key to home cooking, hence Prudence's mum's excellent idea for using up leftovers to make *croquettes*.

Makes about 18

Preparation time: 15 minutes

Cooking time: 25 minutes

250g firm mashed potatoes

100g leftover cooked vegetables, cut into cubes (carrots, parsnips, red pepper, peas) or finely chopped raw broccoli, mushrooms, ham or roast meat, or grated hard cheese (Comté, Cheddar or Gruyère)

salt and freshly ground pepper

10g plain white flour

2 egg whites, beaten until light and foamy

50g dried breadcrumbs

2 tbsp sunflower or vegetable oil

Preheat the oven to 200°C. Mix together the mashed potatoes with your choice of leftovers until well combined. Season with salt and pepper and then roll the mixture into small cylinders that will fit in the palm of your hand.

Set up four plates in front of you. Dust one with the flour, pour the egg whites into another and spread the breadcrumbs on a third. Leave the fourth empty.

Roll the croquettes in the flour, then dip in the egg whites and coat in the breadcrumbs. Place on the clean plate.

Grease a deep baking tray with the oil and heat in the oven for 10 minutes. Remove and carefully add all the *croquettes*. Cook in the oven for 10 minutes before turning over and baking for a further 5 minutes, until crispy and golden brown.

Une petite astuce – tip Be sure to check the seasoning of the *croquette* mixture, as it will depend on the seasoning of your mash and leftovers.

Faire en avance – get ahead The *croquettes* can be made in advance and kept in an airtight container in the fridge for a couple of days or frozen for up to two months.

Soupe à l'oignon et au reglisse avec des chips aux échalotes et fromage

ONION AND LIQUORICE SOUP WITH SHALLOT AND CHEESE CRISPS

Onion soup is one of the most warming and easiest dishes in the French culinary repertoire. Originally a poor man's dish made only with water and onions, a version including croûtons, beef stock and caramelized onions appeared in the seventeenth century. In this recipe I've added my own twists with garlic and liquorice for extra depth. Toss in some small pickled onions at the end if you'd like a little sharpness to cut through the richness.

Serves 4

Preparation time: 30 minutes
Cooking time: 1½ hours

2 spring onions

40g butter

500g onions, peeled and finely sliced

5 cloves of garlic, peeled and minced

1 tsp sugar

½ tsp liquorice powder or
1 tsp fennel seeds

400ml dry white wine

1.5 litres beef or vegetable stock
mixed with ½ tsp Marmite

salt

optional: 12 small pickled onions

For the shallot and cheese crisps

8 shallots

4 thick slices of stale bread, cut into
large 3cm cubes

1 tbsp melted butter

80g mature Comté, Beaufort or other
strongly flavoured cheese, finely grated

Finely chop the spring onions, reserving the green parts for garnish. Melt the butter in a large saucepan over a low heat and add the spring onions, onions and garlic. Cook for about 45 minutes, stirring occasionally to make sure the garlic and onions don't catch on the bottom. When the onions are sticky, soft and a deep golden colour, sprinkle in the sugar and the liquorice or fennel. Continue to stir for a couple more minutes until the onions caramelize. Add the wine and stock, top with the lid, and leave to simmer gently for 45 minutes.

Meanwhile prepare the shallot crisps. Preheat the oven to 190°C and line a baking tray with baking paper. Peel and halve the shallots then separate the layers to create shallot 'leaves'. Toss the shallots with the cubes of bread in the melted butter and spread out over the lined baking tray. Sprinkle the cheese over the top and then cook in the oven for 15 minutes, shaking the tray occasionally. The cheese should be melted and slightly golden on the edges.

Taste the soup and season with salt if required. Pour the soup into serving bowls and top with the crispy shallots and croûtons. Sprinkle with the green bits of spring onion and the pickled onions, if using. Serve immediately (the shallots go soggy in the soup).

Velouté de potimarron avec de la crème Chantilly, des oignons confits et des grains de potimarron

SILKY SMOOTH PUMPKIN SOUP WITH CHANTILLY, ONION CONFIT AND PUMPKIN SEEDS

Onion soup is pretty much a staple on every French alpine menu. But, listed just underneath, a vivacious orange pumpkin soup sometimes appears, looking almost out of place between the drabber winter fare. Roasting the pumpkin might sound like a bit of a palaver but it's well worth it as it takes on a rich sweetness that simply doesn't compare to it being boiled in a pot of stock. The soup is delicious on its own but, to add a little alpine flavour, I've topped it off with some fluffy edible snow (well, almost!). A little whipped cream sprinkled with some caramelized onions and crunchy seeds and you'll have a vibrant and colourful soup for those dark winter days.

Serves 4
Preparation time: 30 minutes
Cooking time: 45 minutes

1kg chestnut pumpkin, pumpkin or butternut squash, chopped into large pieces (reserve the seeds)

4 cloves of garlic, unpeeled and left whole

2 tbsp olive oil

salt

1 large onion, peeled and finely sliced

1 tbsp butter

1 litre hot vegetable stock

freshly ground pepper

100ml whipping cream

Preheat the oven to 180°C. Arrange the pumpkin, garlic and about half of the pumpkin seeds on a baking tray. Toss with the oil and a pinch of salt. Roast for 30 minutes or until tender.

Leave to cool and then scoop out the flesh from the pumpkin pieces into a pot and discard the skin. Squeeze out the garlic flesh from their skins and add to the pot.

Clean the seeds of any strands of pumpkin and place in a separate pan with the onion and butter. Fry over a medium heat for about 10 minutes, stirring occasionally, until the onion begins to caramelize.

Meanwhile, finish the soup by adding the hot stock to the pumpkin and garlic. Blend until smooth using a stick blender, then taste and season with salt and pepper.

Whip the cream with a pinch of salt and plenty of black pepper, to taste. Ladle the soup into serving bowls and top with the whipped cream and the caramelized onions and pumpkin seeds.

Une petite astuce – tip If you're making this soup in advance, you may need to add a little extra stock when you reheat it, as the soup thickens when chilled.

Faire en avance – get ahead The soup can be made several days in advance and kept in the fridge.

Tourte à la saucisse et rognons

SMOKED SAUSAGE AND KIDNEY PIE

Meandering around Lyon I saw countless butchers and delis accessorized with various sausages strung up above the counters – smoked, cured, fresh, fat or skinny. I couldn't resist a couple for the suitcase, although my meaty-smelling clothes probably thought otherwise. Back in my little Paris kitchen, I thought that a Lyonnais twist on the British classic steak and kidney pie would be a great way of using one of my souvenirs.

Serves 4

Preparation time: 30 minutes
Cooking time: 1 hour 30 minutes
Equipment: a pie dish approx. 20cm long and 6cm deep

150g lardons (or smoked bacon), roughly chopped

200g smoked sausage, roughly chopped

6 shallots, peeled and halved

400g veal or lamb kidneys, trimmed of any sinew

2 cloves of garlic, peeled

200g new potatoes, washed

2 carrots, peeled and finely chopped

1 small cooked beetroot, peeled and roughly chopped

500ml red wine

500ml hot veal or beef stock

1 tbsp cornstarch

salt and freshly ground pepper

1 egg, beaten

250g puff pastry

Fry the lardons and smoked sausage in a large pot over a medium to high heat. When the lardons begin to brown and release some of their fat, add the shallots, kidneys and garlic, and cook until the shallots are soft. Add the potatoes, carrots, beetroot, wine and hot stock. Cover and leave to simmer gently for 1 hour.

Place all the meat and vegetables in the pie dish and pour the cooking liquid into another saucepan. Preheat the oven to 180°C.

Mix the cornstarch with some water to make a runny paste. Whisk into the leftover stock over a medium heat, and continue to whisk until it has thickened to the consistency of double cream and started to bubble. Remove from the heat, season with pepper and taste for salt. Pour into the pie dish and brush the edge of the dish with the beaten egg.

Roll out the pastry to a thickness of 5mm and place on top of the pie dish. Press the pastry around the edge to seal. Use a knife to trim off any excess pastry and cut a cross on the top. Brush twice with the beaten egg before cooking in the oven for 15 minutes or until the pastry is golden and puffy.

Une petite astuce – tip A good smoked sausage is essential to give the pie its delicious flavour. *Reflets de France Saucisse de Morteau* is available in good supermarkets.

Faire en avance – get ahead Make the filling a day or two in advance and let it rest in the fridge; it will make for a more flavoursome filling.

Crozets à la truite fumée et petits pois

BUCKWHEAT PASTA DIAMONDS WITH SMOKED TROUT AND PEAS

The Savoie region has spectacular jade green rivers and lakes, which are inhabited by freshwater brown and rainbow trout. Fishing for these prized fish is a popular pastime with locals and tourists alike, and it is well worth bracing the glacier-cold waters to catch them, as the firm sweet flesh offers an excellent antidote to the heavy dishes associated with the region.

Serves 4

Preparation time: 25 minutes
Cooking time: 15 minutes

2 tbsp butter

1 onion, peeled and finely chopped

2 cloves of garlic, peeled and finely chopped

100ml white wine

150g fresh or frozen peas

2 heaped tbsp crème fraîche

freshly ground pepper

150g smoked trout, cut into strips

4 radishes, thinly sliced to garnish

optional: 2 tbsp trout or salmon eggs

For the pasta

200g buckwheat flour, plus extra for dusting

a pinch of salt

2 eggs

60ml milk

To make the buckwheat pasta, mix the flour with the salt in a bowl. Make a well in the middle, crack in the eggs and add the milk. Stir together until you get a lump of dough. Dust the work surface with plenty of flour and divide the dough in half. Take one half and dust it with more flour. Roll it out until it has a thickness of about 2mm then cut into very small diamond shapes (about 5mm). Slide a plastic pastry scraper or plastic card under the pasta to lift it off the surface. Toss it gently to break it up and place on a baking tray that has been lightly dusted with flour. Roll out the second half of the dough and repeat. Bring a large pot of water to a boil.

Meanwhile, place the butter, onion and garlic in a large pan. Cook over a medium heat for 3–4 minutes, until the onions have softened. Add the wine and leave to simmer while you cook the pasta.

When the large pot of water has come to the boil add the peas and pasta. When the pasta floats to the top (roughly 2 minutes) use a slotted spoon to transfer the peas and pasta to the pan with the onions. Stir in the crème fraîche and season with pepper. Remove from the heat before gently mixing through the smoked trout and garnishing with the radishes and trout eggs. Serve immediately.

Salade Savoyarde avec une vinaigrette de noix

CHUNKY SAVOIE SALAD WITH A WALNUT VINAIGRETTE

I love a good salad, especially in the French style, known as *gourmande*. This word has no literal English translation but it evokes gastronomic indulgence and pleasure. Each region in France has their own version of this salad, to showcase the area's ingredients, whether a local ham, cheese or a variety of bean. After a few days of skiing in the French Alps, the crunchy raw textures were a welcome break from the rich foods I had been savouring, such as cheese fondue (see page 213). The version I had was a well-dressed green salad (a good vinaigrette is essential) enriched with *lardons* and Beaufort cheese. Back at home I recreated the flavours, souping-up the salad with a few extras for added textures and tastes. During my stay I came across lots of walnuts, so I have added them to the vinaigrette, and have included apple and some peppery radishes for sweetness and bite. This is really just a hint though; switch and mix up the vegetables to your own taste and based on what's in season.

Serves 4 as a main, or 8 as a side

Preparation time: 20 minutes • Cooking time: 10 minutes

1 small head of leafy lettuce, washed, dried and roughly torn • 10 radishes, thinly sliced • 1 apple, cored and cut into cubes • 1 small cucumber, cut in ribbons using a speed peeler or mandolin • 100g lardons (or bacon, cut into strips) • 2 thick slices of bread, cut into 2cm squares • 100g Beaufort or other strongly flavoured cheese shavings • salt and freshly ground pepper • crusty bread, to serve
For the walnut vinaigrette: 50g walnuts • 50ml sunflower oil • 2 tbsp white wine vinegar • a pinch of salt

First make the vinaigrette. Toast the walnuts in a dry pan until they smell roasted. Chop them finely, then mix with the oil, vinegar and salt.

Toss the lettuce leaves, radishes, apple and cucumber ribbons in the vinaigrette.

Fry the lardons with the croûtons in a large pan until golden. Sprinkle on top of the salad with the cheese shavings. Toss together and season, to taste. Serve immediately with some crusty bread.

Une petite astuce – tip Walnuts can be replaced with other nuts such as pine nuts, pecans or hazelnuts.

Faire en avance – get ahead It's best not to make the salad in advance as the apples will go brown and the croûtons will become soggy.

Haricots savoyard avec lentilles aux herbes

GREEN BEAN BUNDLES WITH HERB LENTIL SALAD

In France, one way of spotting a good bistro from a bad one is by the standard of their *haricots verts*. Spot a dull, limp green bean and it's either come from a tin or has been overcooked; rarely the sign of a good chef at work. Wrap anything in *jambon de Savoie* (a smoky ham) and add a regional cheese, such as Beaufort, and you'll have the essence of the flavours of Savoie at your fingertips. Traditionally veal is stuffed with Beaufort cheese and wrapped in smoky ham, but green beans work just as well.

Serves 4–6
Preparation time: 20 minutes
Cooking time: 30 minutes

salt

400g green beans, trimmed

100g Beaufort or other strongly flavoured hard cheese, cut into thin sticks the length of a green bean

8 slices of smoky ham, speck or Parma ham

200g Puy lentils

1 bay leaf

1 onion, peeled and finely chopped

1 heaped tbsp butter

2 sprigs of thyme, leaves picked

1 heaped tbsp grainy mustard

Preheat the oven to 180°C. Bring a large pot of salted water to the boil, add the beans and boil for 4 minutes or until the beans are cooked but still crunchy. Remove the beans (you can keep the water for boiling the lentils) and run under cold water.

Take a bunch of about ten beans and add a couple of sticks of cheese to the bundle. Wrap a slice of ham tightly around the middle to keep everything together. Place in a baking dish and repeat with the rest of the beans, cheese and ham. Cook in the oven for 20 minutes or until the ham begins to crisp up.

Meanwhile, add the lentils and bay leaf to boiling water. Cook for 15–20 minutes or until the lentils are al dente. Drain and run under cold water to stop the cooking.

Fry the onion with the butter and thyme until soft and translucent. Add the lentils and mustard and stir together. Remove from the heat and serve immediately with the green bean wraps.

Les petits pains au fromage fondu avec une salade de chouxfleur et cornichons

BREAD ROLL FONDUES WITH CAULIFLOWER PICKLE

A trip to the French Alps wouldn't be complete without a pot of fondue with its zingy white wine kick and plenty of bread for dipping. And that's exactly what I wanted, and ate, on my first night. It was the perfect dish to set me up for a day of skiing (my first time on the slopes) the following morning. The combination and ratio of cheeses always varies with each cook boasting their own secret recipe. In general, it's a mix of a local strong cheese, like Beaufort, mellowed out by a milder cheese like Emmental. The classic fondue uses a fondue pot complete with burner, but, unfortunately, there just isn't room for any more kitchen gadgets in my little Paris kitchen, so I came up with an alternative solution. Bread rolls make for the perfect edible pot and offer your guests a warm, golden, oozy surprise.

Serves 6

Preparation time: 15 minutes • Cooking time: 10–15 minutes

1 small head of cauliflower, broken into florets (approx. 400g) • 2 tbsp white wine vinegar (or the pickling vinegar from the cornichons or onions) • 1 heaped tbsp grainy mustard • 2 tbsp sunflower oil • 15 cornichons, roughly chopped • 10 small pickled onions, roughly chopped • salt • 6 medium bread rolls
For the fondue: 1 clove of garlic, peeled • 150ml dry white wine • 1 tsp lemon juice • 150g Beaufort, Gruyère or mature Cheddar cheese, finely grated • 100g Emmental, finely grated

Preheat the oven to 180°C. Bring a large pot of water to the boil and cook the cauliflower florets for 4 minutes or until *al dente*. Drain and run under cold water to stop them cooking.

Mix together the vinegar, mustard and oil, then toss the cauliflower, cornichons and pickled onions in the dressing. Season, to taste, with salt then set aside.

Place the bread rolls in the oven and, while they crisp up, make the fondue. Rub the whole garlic clove around a small saucepan. Add the wine and lemon juice and bring to the boil. Reduce the heat to low and then stir in the cheeses until completely melted. When you have a runny sauce, remove the rolls from the oven. Slice the top off each roll and use your thumb to press down the dough in the middle to create a hollow. Fill with the cheesy sauce and replace the bread lid. Serve immediately, whilst the cheese sauce is hot, with the salad on the side.

Les oeufs au chocolat

CHOCOLATE EGGS

Pâques (Easter) is the ultimate occasion for chef *pâtissiers* to flex their chocolate-making skills. The French like to celebrate with a broad range of chocolate surprises: from cocoa fish and monkeys, through to tree trunks and milkmaid figurines. Traditional themes and simple egg shapes are seen to be for amateurs. A bit of a traditionalist, however, I remain fond of a good old Easter egg, especially these dinky little ones filled with praline.

Makes 6 eggs

Preparation time: 20 minutes
Cooking time: 15 minutes
Setting time: 3 hours
Equipment: 6 x 40cm lengths of ribbon, 1–2cm wide

6 eggs

50g dark chocolate

1 tsp sunflower oil

50g praline (see page 276), chopped pistachios, dehydrated strawberries or raspberries, finely chopped

For the ganache filling

200g dark chocolate, finely chopped

200ml double cream

20g butter, softened

Preheat the oven to 160°C. Use a needle or metal skewer to poke a hole in the bottom of one of the eggs (on the non-pointy side). Wiggle the needle until the hole is 1cm wide. Poke a tiny hole in the opposite side. Blow through the tiny hole to push the egg out the larger hole and into a bowl. Repeat with the rest of the eggs.

Rinse out the egg shells and cook in the oven for 10 minutes to sterilize them. Leave to cool before using.

Melt the 50g of dark chocolate in a heatproof bowl placed over a saucepan of gently simmering water (don't let the base of the bowl touch the water). Stir occasionally, until melted, then stir in the oil. Pour a teaspoon of the melted chocolate into one of the eggshells. Swirl it around and then turn it upside down and leave it to drain in an old egg carton. Repeat with the rest of the eggs.

Make a second layer of chocolate inside each egg, but before leaving it to set, drop a teaspoon of the finely chopped praline inside each one and shake it around so it sticks to the chocolate. Repeat with the rest of the eggs and praline. Leave in the fridge to set for 30 minutes.

To make the ganache, place the chocolate in a heatproof bowl. Bring the cream just to the boil in a saucepan and pour over the chocolate. Leave for 2 minutes and then stir together and add the butter. Pour the ganache into a piping bag with a small nozzle and pipe into the eggs through the larger hole. Shake the egg to release any air bubbles then leave to set in an egg box for several hours at room temperature or in the fridge for 30 minutes. Wrap a bow around the egg to cover the hole at the bottom.

Tarte au chocolat et crème fraîche

CHOCOLATE AND CRÈME FRAÎCHE TART

Bernachon, a chocolate shop in Lyon, selects its own beans, then roasts and grinds them together to create a unique blend. If you're ever in Lyon, be sure to pass by even if it is just to *lèche la vitrine* (lick the window), as the French aptly describe window-shopping. One of their chocolate blends – the *Palais d'Or* (Golden Palace) – made with crème fraîche, happens to translate equally well into a rich and luxurious tart.

Serves 12

Preparation time: 30 minutes

Resting time: 2½ hours

Cooking time: 45 minutes

Equipment: a 23cm round tart tin, 3cm deep, buttered

1 x sweet pastry dough (see page 275)

a knob of butter, for greasing

150g dark chocolate, finely chopped

50g milk chocolate

250g crème fraîche

50ml milk

a pinch of salt

For the chocolate shards

100g dark or white chocolate (or 50g of each)

1 tbsp coconut oil (if using white chocolate)

First make the pastry (see page 275) and set aside to rest. Preheat the oven to 180°C. Roll out the dough between sheets of baking paper until it is 3–5mm thick.

Line the prepared tin with the pastry, trimming away any excess, and prick the base several times with a fork. Place a crumpled sheet of baking paper on top and pour in some baking beans. Cook in the oven for 20 minutes before removing the baking beans and paper. Bake for a further 10 minutes then remove from the oven and leave to cool.

To make the filling, put both the chocolates, the crème fraîche, milk and salt in a heatproof bowl and place it over a pan of gently simmering water (don't let the base of the bowl touch the water). Stir occasionally until melted. Pour the chocolate ganache into the cooked and cooled tart shell and chill for 1½ hours.

In the meantime, make the chocolate shards. Melt the dark chocolate in a heatproof bowl over a pan of gently simmering water, as before. When melted, pour over a large piece of baking paper and spread out evenly and thinly using a spatula. Leave to cool in the fridge and then snap into 5cm shards. Do the same with the white chocolate (if using), adding the coconut oil as the chocolate melts.

When the tart has chilled, remove from the fridge and jab the shards into the surface of the chocolate. If you're not serving immediately, remove it from the fridge anyway and keep in a cool, dark place. The tart is best eaten at room temperature, otherwise the chocolate ganache will be too hard.

Brioche

BRIOCHE

As a child I would eat brioche like it was going out of fashion. There's something so satisfying about the texture: doughy like bread, sweet like cake, and positioned somewhere between naughty and normal. It's unsurprising really; it's essentially a bread pimped up with plenty of butter, eggs and a hit of sweetness.

Makes 1 loaf

Preparation time: 30 minutes using the mixer; 45 minutes by hand (be prepared for a work out)

Resting time: 2¾ hours, or overnight

Cooking time: 30 minutes

Equipment: a 900g loaf tin lined with baking paper

240g strong white flour, plus extra for dusting

25g sugar

5g salt

7g instant dried yeast

70ml milk

2 eggs, plus 1 egg yolk

125g butter, softened and cubed

1 egg yolk mixed with 2 tbsp milk

a small handful of nibbed/pearl sugar (can be bought online or from specialist suppliers)

Place the flour, sugar, salt and yeast in the bowl of a mixer fitted with a dough hook. On a slow speed mix the dry ingredients then add the milk and eggs and continue to mix on a slow speed for 2 minutes. Switch to a medium speed for a further 6–8 minutes. The dough will become soft, smooth and elastic.

Add the cubes of softened butter piece by piece and continue to mix until the butter is thoroughly combined (roughly another 5 minutes). Scrape the bowl down periodically with a spatula to ensure all the butter is incorporated. Tip the dough into a bowl, cover with cling film and chill for at least 2 hours or overnight.

Lightly dust the work surface and your hands with flour. Tip out the dough and knead for a minute before shaping into a sausage shape that fits into the loaf tin. Pop into the prepared tin, seam side down, and brush with the egg wash. Leave to rise in a warm place for 45 minutes or until it doubles in size. Do not leave it anywhere too hot, as the butter in the brioche will start to melt.

Preheat the oven to 180°C. Brush the brioche with more egg wash and sprinkle with the nibbed sugar. Cook in the oven for 30 minutes or until a skewer inserted into the middle comes out clean. Cover the brioche with foil if it's browning too quickly.

Remove from the oven and leave to cool for 5 minutes before taking it out of the tin and placing on a wire rack to cool.

Brioche à la praline

PRALINE BRIOCHE

Bright pink, sugar-coated almonds are the star ingredient in Lyonnais patisserie. Unlike classic praline, Lyonnais praline is not caramelized. Instead, the sugar is heated and left snow white to be dyed bright pink. Lyonnais praline is sold in packets and can be eaten on its own, but often it is spotted on tarts, cakes and desserts. I think the best way of eating it is when paired with a soft buttery brioche. This recipe makes double the amount of praline needed for the brioche, in case you subscribe to my method of cooking, which involves a lot of tasting along the way (you can store the rest in an airtight container).

Makes 1 loaf

Preparation time: 30 minutes using the mixer, 45 minutes by hand

Resting time: 45 minutes

Cooking time: 45 minutes

Equipment: a 900g loaf tin, lined with baking paper; sugar thermometer

1 x portion of basic brioche dough (see opposite page)

flour, to dust

1 egg yolk mixed with 2 tbsp milk

For the rose praline

40ml water

200g sugar

100g shelled almonds, blanched and skinless

For the second coating

40ml water

200g sugar

a tube of good-quality red food colouring gel* (see page 221)

Make the brioche dough then keep it in the fridge while you make the rose praline. Line a baking tray with baking paper. Pour the water into a saucepan with the sugar and bring to the boil. Don't stir, but gently swirl the pan until the sugar dissolves. Use a sugar thermometer and when it reaches 135°C (the hard-ball stage), remove from the heat and stir in the almonds. Continue to stir until the sugar has a sandy texture. Pour on to the lined baking tray and leave to cool. Pick out and discard any lumps of sugar.

When the almonds are almost cool, bring the second batch of water and sugar – this time with the food colouring added – to 135°C. Quickly stir in the nuts so they are coated in the sugar and then immediately tip them back out on to the lined baking tray. Too much stirring will make the sugar sandy, but do make sure each almond is coated individually in the pink sugar. Leave to cool before roughly chopping 100g (and storing the rest in an airtight container).

Remove the brioche dough from the fridge. Dust the work surface and the top of the dough with flour then roll it out to a square, roughly 40cm x 40cm. Move the dough around from time to time to make sure it's not sticking to the work surface (dust with more flour if needed).

Cut the dough into 16 equal squares. Brush each one with egg wash and sprinkle with the chopped praline (keep a little for sprinkling at the end). Lay the squares loosely against one another in the lined loaf tin, slotting them side-by-side like books on a shelf, filling the tin two-thirds full. You might find it easier with the tin on its side.

Brush with egg wash and leave to rise in a warm (but not too hot) place for 45 minutes or until the dough has risen by a few centimetres and looks puffy.

Preheat the oven to 180°C. Carefully egg wash the brioche and sprinkle with the remaining praline. Bake for 30 minutes** or until a skewer inserted into the middle comes out clean. Leave to cool for 5 minutes before turning out on to a wire rack.

Les petites astuces – tips *Now available in most supermarkets. Avoid buying the cheap liquid, as it usually takes using a whole bottle to get a decent colour. If you can't find the gel, then use a coloured powder.

**Check on the brioche in the last 15 minutes of cooking time. You may need to cover it with a piece of foil if it's looking too brown on top before its fully cooked in the centre.

You can also use chocolate chips. Simply replace the praline with 75g dark chocolate chips.

Faire en avance – get ahead The praline can be made in advance. It will keep in an airtight container in a cool, dark place for months.

Tarte aux noix, sarrasin et caramel salé

WALNUT AND BUCKWHEAT CARAMEL TART

Grenoble is not only known for being the capital of the Alps, but also for its walnuts which were awarded with an AOC label, making them the most sought after in France. When the season arrives, the vegetable man at my local market in Paris will have a box of them for sale. I am not going to lie: they are a bit of a pain to crack open but luckily for the time-pressed, it's possible to buy them already shelled. Walnuts have a slight bitter note that works particularly well with sweet and salty caramel, and the toasted buckwheat grains add an additional crunch.

Makes 1 tart
Preparation time: 30 minutes
Resting time: 1 hour
Cooking time: 45 minutes
Equipment: an 11cm x 35cm tart tin, buttered

1 x shortcrust pastry dough
(see page 274)

For the filling

250g walnuts, toasted

150g buckwheat, toasted
(see page 30)

150g sugar

100ml double cream

40g golden syrup or molasses

40g butter

½ tsp salt

First, make your pastry (see page 274) and leave it to rest in the fridge for at least an hour. Preheat the oven to 180°C. Roll out the dough between 2 sheets of baking paper until 3–5mm thick.

Line the tin with the pastry and prick the base several times with a fork. Place a sheet of baking paper on top and pour in some baking beans. Cook in the oven for 20 minutes before removing the baking beans and paper and baking for a further 10 minutes. Remove from the oven and leave to cool slightly before removing the pastry case from the tin.

To make the caramel, put half the sugar in a pot with 2 tablespoons of water. Place over a high heat and leave to melt. Do not stir, but swirl the pot around if needed. Once the caramel becomes a dark reddish brown colour, remove it from the heat and add the rest of the filling ingredients. Be careful not to stand over the pan, as the caramel will steam and bubble. Swirl the pan around before returning to a medium heat. Cook for 3–4 minutes or until it reaches 113°C.

Stir in the nuts and buckwheat and then pour immediately into the pastry case. Spread out the filling and leave for 10 minutes to set at room temperature before serving.

Alsace

LA TERRINE À BAECKEOFFE

LE BRETZEL

LE KOUGELHOPF

LES KNACKS

LE CHRISTKINDELSMÄRIK

ALSACE

STRASBOURG

ALLEMAGNE

LA WINSTUB

LES MAENNELES

LA FACHWARIKHÜS

LES VOSGES

LA ROUTE DU VIN D'ALSACE

COLMAR

RHEIN

LA COSTUME ALSACIENNE

LES BREDELE

LE GEWÜRZTRAMINER

MULHOUSE

SUISSE

LE FROMAGE BLANC

LE STORCK

LA BIERE

LA CHOUCROUTE

CINNAMON SPICE, FESTIVE DELIGHTS
AND LOTS OF ICE

Perhaps it was the wood-beamed architecture, love of sausage and wafting smells of sweet spiced cakes that meant Alsace, out of all the regions I visited, felt the most familiar to me, despite having never visited it before.

Alsace lies in the northeastern corner of France, with Germany bordering to the north and east, and Switzerland to the south. Its location has resulted in a unique blend of cultures, drawing influences from all its neighbours, especially Germany. I had eaten some of the typical Alsacian cuisine, like sauerkraut with smoked sausage – its most famous export. Many other dishes, such as *spätzle*, *kugelhopf* (see pages 254–9) and *bredele* (see pages 266 and 270), used flavours I recognized from spending my teenage years growing up in Bavaria in Germany.

I headed to Alsace a week before Christmas and it turned out to be the busiest time of the year to visit, with its famous Christmas markets in full swing. The air was filled with a heady mix of *vin chaud aux épices* (mulled spiced wine), candied nuts and pine needles. Christmas trees and twigs decorate the outside of cute, little wooden huts, delicately draped with bright twinkling lights.

When evening descends, the markets truly come to life, with people sipping hot mulled wine and munching on sausages, *bretzel* or some of the many sweet treats on offer, including waffles, crêpes and a wonderful array of Christmas biscuits. In Strasbourg, the region's capital, I found a market that had a handful of stands run by local producers. One was selling goat's cheese, another showcasing artisan beer, a local mushroom grower offered a selection of dried and fresh mushrooms and a flour miller artisanal flours and biscuits . . . All of them were warm and welcoming in spite of the finger-numbing cold weather (wrapping your hands around a warm cup of *vin chaud* is a must at all times).

Luckily, the action doesn't just take place outside. There's plenty to discover inside too. The Alsacians have their version of a bistro, the *winstub*, although it is a little less grand than the ones you see in Paris. Think wooden chairs with little hearts carved out in the back, red-and-white checked tablecloths and a generally heartwarming atmosphere. Portions are generous, definitely not for the fainthearted. *Choucroute garnie, baeckehoffe* (see page 247) and *flammekueche*, a sort of pizza made with crème fraîche, onion and bacon, are never off the menu, no matter whether it's freezing cold outside or the height of summer. The bakeries are delightful, with the famous *kugelhopf* in various sizes on display (see page 254); around Christmas-time most of them will bring out an amazing assortment of biscuits, (see pages 266 and 270). Chocolate shops are crammed with goodies, like confit-covered chestnuts and plenty of marzipan figures.

If sweets aren't your thing, make sure to pop by a butcher (I recommend Frick Lutz in Strasbourg) for a huge selection of cold meats and sausages. What we would see as a Frankfurter or hotdog sausage is something of a specialty here. But do not think that all hotdog sausages are the same; there's a reason why the locals call them *'le knack'*: a good one will snap loudly. With your sausage you'll need some beer, of course. Alsacians love their beer and there are plenty of brasseries in which to drink a pint or two (I even found one in Strasbourg, at micro brasserie l a Lanterne, which brewed its own).

Despite the damage caused by the bombing during the Second World War, most of the cities and towns in the area have managed to keep their original architecture: buildings with exposed wooden beams and shutters painted in pastel colours, and during the summer months window boxes planted with colourful flowers flowing over the sides. Colmar is particularly renowned for its picturesque architecture, making it a popular destination for busloads of tourists. It's almost Disney-esque and a bit too perfect for my liking, but still well worth a visit.

As you head out of the urban areas towards the mountains, nature takes over. Buildings become a little more 'lived in' and rural. *Le route du vin*, an attraction just as famous as the Christmas markets, runs from the north to the south of Alsace and celebrates the region's long winemaking tradition that dates back to when the Romans invaded Alsace and made it their centre of viticulture. Some of the famous local wines include Riesling, Gewürztraminer, Sylvaners and Muscat – all of which are enjoying a revival of late.

Alsace had me utterly charmed. Deciding what recipes to feature, twist or simply convey in their classic form for this chapter was far from an easy task. I decided to include some aromatic edible gifts, both a classic *kugelhopf* and one with a savoury twist (see pages 254 and 258), a hearty glazed ham hock for sharing with friends in the cold months (see page 241), and cute little coconut snowballs inspired by the winter weather (see page 265).

Knepfles à l'épeautre avec Munster et feuilles d'oignons

BUTTON DUMPLINGS WITH MUNSTER CHEESE AND ONION PETALS

Not far from Strasbourg, the capital of Alsace, lies the Moulin de Hurtigheim, a small family-run flour mill and one of the last independently owned mills in the region. It was fascinating to learn about the different grains used to produce particular flours, and see the flour truck which goes round the villages selling flour directly to locals. This dish has its origins in the German word for 'small button' and, although these tiny dumplings can be made with regular white flour, I find spelt adds a certain nuttiness. Perfect with sweet onions and the local Munster cheese. Equally delicious served with a pasta sauce or in a soup.

Serves 2 as a main course
Preparation time: 25 minutes
Resting time: 30 minutes
Cooking time: 30 minutes

125g spelt flour

½ tsp salt

1 egg, beaten

125g fromage blanc or quark

1 red onion

1 tbsp butter

1 tbsp brown sugar

2 tbsp red wine vinegar

salt and freshly ground pepper

50g Munster cheese, sliced, or other strongly flavoured soft cheese (e.g. Camembert or Brie)

Mix together the flour and salt in a bowl and make a well in the middle. Pour in the beaten egg and the fromage blanc and mix together until you have a smooth dough. Place the dough in a piping bag, or use a freezer bag and snip off the corner to make a 1cm opening.

Line a baking tray with baking paper and pipe thick lines of dough across the paper. Place the tray of piped dough in the freezer for 30 minutes.

In the meantime, prepare the red onion. Preheat the oven to 200°C and line a baking tray with foil. Peel the onion, then halve lengthways and trim the root. Cut each half into thirds lengthways. Carefully pull away the individual layers of the onion right up to the heart; you will be left with lots of little onion petals. Add them to the baking tray, toss with the butter, sugar and vinegar, and season with salt and pepper. Cook in the oven for 30 minutes.

Remove the tray from the freezer and cut the dough strips into 5mm rectangles to make your knepfles. A knife dipped in hot water may help.

Bring a large pot of water to the boil over a medium to high heat. Drop the knepfles into the boiling water and when they float to the top they are cooked. Drain in a colander and toss with the red onion leaves. Top with a layer of cheese and serve immediately.

Strasbourg

Frites Alsaciennes au bibelaskäs

ALSACIAN FRIES WITH BIBELASKÄS

When I visited my first traditional Alsacian restaurant, I had a serious case of food envy. Despite how delicious my *bouchée à la reine* was (see page 233), I couldn't resist pinching some of my dining partner, Marie's, *bibelaskäs* – luscious, thick fresh cheese. It had several accompaniments on the side: finely chopped shallots, little spring-onion rounds and clusters of chopped aromatic herbs. A pile of hot and crunchy potatoes quickly followed, presenting themselves as perfect dunking devices. Luckily, Marie was kind enough to share her recipe for this lighter version of cheesy chips, a recipe which combines her love for her hometown of Strasbourg, with her new home, New York City.

Serves 4
Preparation time: 15 minutes
Cooking time: 20 minutes

1kg potatoes, unpeeled (a waxy variety, like Charlotte or Cyprus)

4 tbsp olive oil

salt

500g fromage blanc or quark

freshly ground pepper

a small bunch of chives, finely chopped

2 shallots, peeled and finely chopped

2 small spring onions, finely chopped

a small bunch of flat-leaf parsley, finely chopped

a small bunch of coriander, finely chopped

Preheat the oven to 200°C. Wash and dry the potatoes. Cut them lengthways into slim 1cm chips, leaving the skin on and then place in a large saucepan of cold water. Bring the water to the boil over a medium heat and as soon as it starts boiling, cook the fries for exactly 1 minute and then drain through a colander. They should still be uncooked and firm to the touch at this point. Place some kitchen towel on a large chopping board, arrange the fries on top and blot them dry.

Line a baking tray with baking paper. Tip the fries on to the tray, pour over the oil and mix to coat. Season with salt then spread them out in a single layer. Cook for 20 minutes, checking on them after 10 minutes and turning them over so they brown evenly.

Divide the fromage blanc between 4 small bowls and season each with salt and pepper. When the fries come out of the oven, season with salt and sprinkle with the chopped chives. Divide between new bowls.

Place bowls of the shallots, spring onions and herbs on the table, along with the bowls of *bibelaskäs* and fries for everyone to help themselves.

Bouchées à la reine végétarienne

VEGETABLE PASTRY PUFFS

During lunch at a cosy *winstub* (a traditional Alsacian restaurant), I spotted a dish at a neighbouring table and immediately knew it was the one for me. It was a giant golden puff-pastry frame, filled to the brim with dumplings, chicken and a creamy sauce. You are probably wondering where the dumplings and chicken are in my recipe! Well, after a week in hearty and carnivorous Alsace, I arrived back to my little Paris kitchen craving vegetables, and so I decided to swap the meat for some vibrant green broccoli and cauliflower. If you think you would prefer the classic version, you can replace some of the vegetables with leftover roast chicken.

Serves 4

Preparation time: 15 minutes
Cooking time: 35 minutes

375g puff pastry, at room temperature

1 egg mixed with 2 tbsp milk

200g broccoli, cut into evenly sized florets

200g cauliflower, cut into evenly sized florets

For the sauce

30g butter

30g plain white flour

400ml hot vegetable stock

zest of ½ a lemon

100ml Riesling, or other dry white wine

4 tbsp double cream

1 tsp lemon juice

a pinch of sugar

salt and freshly ground pepper

Preheat the oven to 180°C. Line a baking tray with baking paper. Roll out the puff pastry between 2 sheets of baking paper to a thickness of 5mm. Using a sharp knife, cut the pastry into 4 rectangles, each about 13cm x 10cm. Place the pastry pieces on the baking tray, leaving a little space between each one. Using a knife, lightly score a border, 1cm in from the edge. Brush with egg wash and cook in the oven for 15 minutes until golden brown and well risen.

Meanwhile steam the broccoli and cauliflower florets until just tender. Remove the pastry from the oven, gently cut along the scored border and pull out a few layers from the inside to create room for the filling.

To make the sauce, melt the butter in a large saucepan over a medium heat. Add the flour and beat hard until you have a smooth paste. Continue to beat until the roux begins to turn golden. Remove from the heat and gradually add the hot stock and lemon zest, whisking constantly.

Return the pan to the heat and simmer gently for 10 minutes, whisking frequently to ensure the sauce doesn't stick to the bottom of the pan. If the sauce becomes too thick, whisk in a little more stock or water.

Add the wine and simmer for a further 10 minutes, then remove from the heat and whisk in the cream, lemon juice and sugar. Season, to taste, with salt and pepper. Add the vegetables to the pastry *bouchée* and ladle over plenty of the sauce. Serve immediately.

Crackers aux grains de carvi et pomme

CARAWAY AND APPLE CRACKERS

The influence of nearby Germany has introduced darker, more wholesome flours to the Alsace region, like rye and wholemeal. Rye flour marries beautifully with caraway – another local favourite – so I've brought the two together in these rustic biscuits. A hint of apple adds a welcome sweetness. Be warned, these aren't your average cardboard crackers; I could easily munch my way through a batch of these fresh from the oven. If they make it past the fresh-out-of-the-oven munching stage, try serving these on a cheeseboard.

Makes 8 large crackers (with off-cuts)

Preparation time: 15 minutes

Resting time: 1 hour

Cooking time: 20 minutes

Equipment: (optional) a small heart-shaped biscuit cutter

200g rye flour, plus extra for dusting

½ tbsp caraway seeds

3g instant dry yeast

½ tsp salt

a pinch of sugar

1 Granny Smith apple (approx 150g), unpeeled, cored and roughly grated

80ml warm water

Mix together all the dry ingredients with the grated apple. Pour in the water and mix until you have a sticky ball. Cover the bowl with a clean wet tea towel and leave to rest in a warm place for an hour.

Preheat the oven to 180°C. Line two baking trays with baking paper and dust the work surface with flour.

Divide the dough in half and roll out to a thickness of about 3mm (you may need to dust the dough with flour if it is a bit sticky).

Cut into rectangles, roughly 13cm x 9cm. Cut out the centre of each one with the heart-shaped cutter to make them look like the shutters on traditional Alsacian houses (optional). Use a brush to dust off any excess flour then place them on the lined baking trays. Repeat with the other half of the dough. Bake for 20 minutes or until the crackers are crisp. If cooking the cut-out hearts as well, these will only take a couple of minutes. Leave to cool on a wire rack.

Les petites astuces – tips The caraway seeds can be omitted or replaced with other seeds like poppy or sunflower.

A pear would work well instead of the apple, or even a very thinly sliced red onion.

Faire en avance – get ahead The crackers will keep in an airtight container for several weeks.

Pad Alsacien

ALSACIAN NOODLES

Alsace food is hearty fare so I soon found myself craving something crunchy and fresh. Alsacian egg noodles reminded me of those used in the classic Thai street food dish: pad Thai. And so, using local ingredients, the pad Alsace was born. Cabbage and carrots add the crunch, lardons provide some lip-smacking saltiness and, for heat, I've used freshly grated horseradish.

Serves 4
Preparation time: 15 minutes
Cooking time: 10 minutes

4 tbsp runny honey

6 tbsp white wine vinegar

salt

300g Alsacian flat noodles or flat egg noodles

2 tbsp sunflower oil

200g smoked lardons

2 carrots, peeled and cut into matchsticks

¼ of a red cabbage, halved, cored and finely sliced

200g chestnut mushrooms, wiped and quartered

4 shallots, peeled and finely sliced

4 cloves of garlic, peeled and finely chopped

2 spring onions, white and green parts separated, finely sliced

2 heaped tbsp finely grated fresh horseradish

Stir together the honey, vinegar and salt, to taste, and set aside.

Bring a large pot of water to the boil and cook the noodles according to the packet instructions. Drain, reserving a little of the cooking liquid.

Heat the oil in a wok or large frying pan over a high heat until smoking hot. Add the lardons, carrots, cabbage, mushrooms and noodles and stir-fry for 2 minutes. Add the shallots, garlic and the white parts of the spring onions. Continue to fry for a further 2 minutes before adding the honey sauce and a couple of tablespoons of the noodle cooking liquid. Turn the heat off and mix in the horseradish. Serve immediately with the green parts of the spring onion sprinkled on top.

Les petites astuces – tips You can use almost any vegetable you have in the fridge: peppers, courgettes, aubergines, broccoli . . . just make sure to cut them finely, so they cook quickly.

If you can't find fresh horseradish, use 1 tablespoon of jarred grated horseradish.

Jambonneau à la bière

BEER-DOUSED HAM HOCK

Alsace is not only the land of Gewürtzraminer, Riesling and Grüner Veltliner wines, it's also famous for another alcoholic offering: beer. Strasbourg has many brasseries (the word actually means 'brewery') that serve beer and food, but few that actually brew beer on site. I visited one small brewery in Strasbourg called La Lanterne, where they brew everything from your classic blonde to more unusual beers spiked with cinnamon. While I hardly need to state the merits of drinking beer, it also does a pretty good job of marinating and tenderizing meat. The Alsacian love of beer and pork is showcased in this popular brasserie dish.

Serves 4–6

Preparation time: 10–15 minutes
Resting time: 2 hours, or overnight
Cooking time: 3½ – 4 hours

2 ham hocks (each weighing approx. 1.2kg) or 4 small ones*

1.5 litres blonde beer

80g salt, plus extra to season

zest of 1 lemon, plus 2 tbsp juice

10 black peppercorns

4 tbsp runny honey

4 tbsp Dijon mustard

2 onions, peeled and quartered

4 carrots, peeled and sliced lengthways

1 stick of celery, cut in half

250g Puy or green lentils

a small bunch of fresh parsley, leaves only, finely chopped

Score the skin of the ham hocks with a sharp knife. Pour 1.25 litres of the beer and 750ml water into a large bowl and stir in the 80g salt until it has completely dissolved. Add the lemon zest and peppercorns. Submerge the ham hocks in the brine, making sure they are completely covered. Cover with cling film and refrigerate for at least 2 hours, and preferably overnight.

Preheat the oven to 180°C. Remove the ham hocks from the brine. Stir the honey and mustard together and rub it all over the ham hocks.

Place the onions, carrots and celery in a large roasting dish and top with the ham hocks. Pour over 250ml water and the remaining 250ml of beer. Cover with a layer of baking paper, followed by a layer of foil. Cook in the oven for 3½–4 hours, basting the meat regularly with the juices and turning the hocks around from time to time. The meat should be falling off the bone. For the last 30 minutes of the cooking time, remove the foil from the ham.

Meanwhile cook the lentils according to the packet instructions. Drain and toss with the parsley, lemon juice and a pinch of salt.

Serve the lentils with the shredded ham, carrots and onions and some of the roasting juices poured over the top.

Les petites astuces – tips *If you're cooking four smaller ham hocks (each weighing roughly 600g) they will need 2½–3 hours in the oven.

If you can only get salted ham hocks, rinse them in cold water before adding to the beer marinade and leave out the salt.

Chaussons au jambon et légumes

HAM AND VEGETABLE PASTRY PUFFS

Maison Naegel is an iconic bakery in Strasbourg. I was lucky enough to get a behind-the-scenes tour to witness how they make their legendary *kugelhopf* (see my recipes on pages 254 and 258) but they are also famous for their *tourte*, a pie filled with a Béchamel sauce, ham and mushrooms. With some tasty leftovers from my beer-doused ham hock (see page 241) burning a hole in my fridge, it was only a matter of putting two and two together to arrive at this glorious pastry puff. You can adjust or replace the filling to your liking.

Serves 4

Preparation time: 10 minutes

Cooking time: 45 minutes

500g puff pastry, at room temperature

250g ham

100g mature Comté or other strongly flavoured cheese, cut into 1cm chunks

1 boiled potato, chopped into 1cm chunks

2 cooked carrots, chopped into 1cm chunks

2 spring onions, chopped into 1cm pieces

1 egg mixed with 2 tbsp milk

400g thick, cold Béchamel sauce or make some fresh (see page 276)

First make the Béchamel sauce. Preheat the oven to 200°C. Line a baking tray with baking paper. Roll out the puff pastry between sheets of baking paper to a thickness of 3mm. Use a dessert plate (about 16cm in diameter) to cut out 4 rounds.

Mix together all of the remaining ingredients apart from the egg wash. Divide between the pastry rounds, placing the mixture on one side. Be careful not to overfill and to leave at least 1cm around the edge. Brush egg wash all around the edges of the pastry, then fold over the pastry so you have a half-moon shape. Use a fork or your finger to press down the pastry around the edge to seal. Prick the top with a fork and brush with egg wash. You can use the leftover pastry to cut out decorations to stick on to your *chausson*. Bake for 30 minutes, until the bases are golden brown.

Serve warm as a snack or with a salad as a light lunch. They can also be eaten cold.

Les petites astuces – tips Use any leftover cooked meat, poached fish or vegetables – leeks, cheese and potatoes make for a good combination. Just make sure to use a vegetable that isn't too juicy, and if it takes a long time to cook (like pumpkin), be sure to pre-cook it.

Faire en avance – get ahead These can be assembled in advance and frozen for a couple of months in an airtight container (don't brush with egg wash before freezing). They will take a little longer to bake from frozen.

Mikaël Rochel, beef producer at Ferme des Fougères

Baeckehoffe

BAKER'S STEW

This dish is a one-pot wonder where you bung everything into a pot and leave it to simmer away. The story goes that on laundry day, wives would send their husbands and children off to work and school in the morning with the uncooked dish to drop off at the baker's. The baker would pop it into the cooler part of the oven where it would slowly cook until being picked up by either the husband or children on their way home. The lid of the dish would be sealed with dough to keep out any fingers, so nothing got nibbled before it hit the dinner table!

Traditionally, this was made with a mix of lamb, pork and beef, as well as a pig's trotter. The trick is to make sure to include some meat still on the bone; it will add flavour, and a lovely silky texture to the stock.

Serves 6

Preparation time: 15 minutes
Resting time: overnight
(or 24–48 hours)
Cooking time: 3–4 hours

4 beef cheeks

4 slices of oxtail (approx. 800g)

4 thick slices of smoked bacon (approx. 160g)

750ml Riesling wine

2 onions, peeled and quartered

3 carrots, peeled and halved lengthways

4 tomatoes, scored, blanched in boiling water and skinned

10 black peppercorns

500ml water

2 large potatoes, peeled and cut into 2mm-thick slices

500g butternut squash or pumpkin, peeled and cut into 2mm-thick slices

a pinch of salt

Place the meat and the wine in a large container, making sure the meat is fully submerged. Cover with a lid or some cling film and leave to marinate in the fridge overnight (or for a day or two).

Preheat the oven to 160°C. Put the meat, onions, carrots, tomatoes and peppercorns in a large flameproof stew pot with a lid. Pour over the water and wine. Try to create an even surface with no big gaps; this will make it easier to top with the slices of potato and butternut squash.

Neatly and tightly line up alternating rounds of potato and squash around the edge of the pot. The layers should begin to look like petals on a flower. Lay the remaining slices over the top to cover the stew. Sprinkle with salt.

Place a sheet of baking paper on top followed by the lid. Cook in the oven for 3–4 hours. Remove the lid and baking paper and grill for 5–10 minutes to crisp up the potatoes and squash. Serve immediately.

Faire en avance – get ahead This stew is even better cooked the day before and reheated (omit the grilling during the initial cooking). Reheat for 45 minutes at 160°C with the lid on, then remove the lid and grill for 5–10 minutes.

In the Vosges mountains

Soupe au jambonneau et légumes

HAM HOCK AND VEGETABLE SOUP

The backbone of regional French cooking is its resourceful use of ingredients; celebrating lesser cuts, using every single part of the animal and making a little go a long way. This soup is a celebration of leftovers, but that's not to say isn't worthy of making from scratch (see tips).

Serves 4–6

Preparation time: 30 minutes
Cooking time: 30 minutes

200g pearl barley, farro or spelt, rinsed

1 tbsp butter

2 carrots, peeled and chopped into 1cm chunks

2 celery sticks, chopped into 1cm chunks

1 onion, peeled and finely chopped

4 spring onions, trimmed, green and white parts separated, finely chopped

2 tbsp grainy mustard

1.5 litres ham or chicken stock

250g cooked lean ham hock, cut into small chunks

salt and freshly ground pepper

1 pear, cut into 2mm matchsticks

1 tbsp cider vinegar

Cook your chosen grain according to the packet instructions.

Melt the butter in a large saucepan and add the carrots, celery, onion and the green parts of the spring onions. Cook the vegetables for about 10 minutes, until tender but not coloured, then stir in the mustard.

Add in the stock, followed by the ham and cooked pearl barley, and bring to a simmer. Season with salt and pepper, to taste, and divide between serving bowls. Garnish with the white pieces of spring onion.

Put the pieces of pear in a small dish and pour over the cider vinegar (do this just before serving the soup). Serve the pickled pear on the side, for popping it on top of the soup.

Une petite astuce – tip If making this from scratch, boil a ham hock in a large pan of salted water with a carrot, onion, celery stick, a few peppercorns and a couple of bay leaves. Simmer for about 3 hours, until the meat is soft and the broth is tasty. Then follow the recipe as above.

Faire en avance – get ahead This soup will keep in a container in the fridge for a couple of days.

Choux farcis sans saucisse

VEGETARIAN CABBAGE PARCEL

The French are blessed with some of the finest freshly-grown produce. Despite this abundance, most dishes on the French menu will find a way of sneaking in a little something meaty, whether a sprinkling of lardons in a salad or a bit of sausage meat tucked into a tomato. Cabbage leaves make perfect flexible cases for holding flavourful stuffing ingredients so here is my meat-free version – a great vegetarian dish to serve at Christmas.

Serves 4

Preparation time: 30 minutes • Cooking time: 55 minutes

1 Savoy cabbage • 4 tbsp olive oil, plus extra to drizzle • 1 red onion, peeled and finely sliced • 2 cloves of garlic, peeled and crushed • 6 large sage leaves • salt and freshly ground pepper • 50g seedless raisins • 100g cooked and peeled chestnuts (in tins or packets), roughly chopped • 1 apple, cored and roughly cubed • 240g sweet potato, baked in its skin (approx. 400g uncooked) • 2 tbsp red wine vinegar • zest of 1 lemon • 100g Munster cheese or a goat's cheese log, broken into chunks

Peel away the very tough external leaves of the cabbage and cut out the tough inner core. Bring a large pan of water to the boil and place the cabbage, stem side up, into the water. Cook for 5–10 minutes, until soft but still holding together. Remove from the water and leave to cool slightly. Peel off about 10 loose outer leaves and set these aside. Finely chop the tighter part of the head.

Preheat the oven to 180°C. Heat the oil in a large frying pan over a low to medium heat and add the onion, garlic and 5 chopped sage leaves and season with salt. Cook gently for 5 minutes, until soft. Add the chopped cabbage, and cook for 3 minutes.

Add the raisins, chestnuts, apple and sweet potato with the vinegar and 2 tablespoons of water to loosen. Remove from the heat, stir in the lemon zest and cheese. Season with salt and pepper.

Take two 50cm lengths of butcher's string and place them to form a cross in the base of a deep bowl, with the ends draped over the side. Place a couple of cabbage leaves on top of the string, overlapping them to create a nest for the filling. Spoon all the filling into the centre of the leaves, then layer more leaves around the edges to overlap the bottom leaves, tucking them in and around the sides and covering the top of the filling.

When the filling is well enveloped by the cabbage leaves, tie the strings together tightly on top in a neat bow, with a sage leaf tucked underneath. Place the cabbage parcel on a baking tray lined with baking paper, sprinkle with a little salt and a drizzle with oil. Cook in the oven for 30 minutes.

Serve the cabbage as a centrepiece and cut into wedges at the table.

Kugelhopf

KUGELHOPF

I was a woman on a mission when I visited Alsace. I had heard a lot about the famous *kugelhopf* and was in search of the ultimate version. I taste-tested the classic ones speckled with raisins, others accessorized with *tagada* (strawberry-flavoured sweets), some studded with chocolate, and plenty of savoury ones spiked with bacon. During my extensive kugelhopf research I discovered that the best ones were very light and moist and made with the juiciest of raisins.

Kugelhopfs are typically baked in a ring-shaped mould called a *kugelhopf*, but if you don't have one, a loaf tin works well too. The traditional Alsacian version is very similar to a brioche, made with yeast and enriched with butter and egg. My version is a little less buttery than its brioche cousin (see page 218) but it's just as moreish. I've opted for lovely squidgy prunes to stud mine, but you can easily make the classic version with raisins or any other dried fruit you may have at home. See a photograph of the finished cake on page 256.

Serves 8
Preparation time: 45 minutes • Resting time: 6 hours, or preferably overnight • Cooking time: 30 minutes
Equipment: a 20cm kugelhopf mould or a 900g loaf tin

300g strong white bread flour • 40g sugar • 1 tsp table salt • 5g instant dried yeast • 125ml milk • 1 egg, beaten • 70g butter, softened and cut into small cubes, plus 1 tbsp for greasing • optional: 8–10 blanched almonds, for decoration • 70g pitted soft prunes • optional: 50ml Cognac, rum or brandy (if using very dry prunes or other dried fruit)* • 1 egg mixed with 2 tbsp milk

Mix together all the dry ingredients in the bowl of a food processor fitted with a dough hook. Make a well in the middle and pour in the milk and egg. Mix on a medium speed for 6–8 minutes, until the dough is soft, smooth and elastic.

Add the softened butter, bit by bit, and continue to mix for about 5 minutes, until the butter is thoroughly incorporated. Scrape the bowl with a spatula to ensure all the butter is mixed in.

Once a dough has formed (it should be slightly sticky), transfer it to a large clean bowl. Cover with cling film and leave in the fridge until it has doubled in size (ideally overnight).

Grease the kugelhopf mould with the tablespoon of butter. If using a loaf tin, line it with baking paper but do not grease it. Place an almond in each groove of the mould; if using a loaf tin, just scatter the almonds loosely over the base.

Drain the prunes of any excess liquid (if they were soaked in Cognac) and lightly knead them into the dough, keeping kneading to a minimum.

Shape the dough into a ball and poke a hole through the middle. Tuck it neatly into the mould, making sure the middle of the mould is peeking through the dough and brush with egg wash. If using a loaf tin, shape the dough into a sausage shape the length of the tin. Pop the dough into the tin and brush with egg wash. Cover with a clean damp tea towel or cling film and leave somewhere warm to rise to double its size.

Preheat the oven to 200°C. Brush the kugelhopf with more egg wash and bake for 30 minutes, or until a skewer inserted into the middle comes out clean.

Remove from oven and leave to cool for 10 minutes before turning out on to a wire rack.

Les petites astuces – tips *If using dried prunes, cut them into 1cm chunks and soak them in the Cognac overnight, or for at least the same amount of time the dough needs to rise in the fridge. It's important to leave the fruit plenty of time to soak up the alcohol as this will make it juicy. If you prefer not to use alcohol, freshly squeezed orange juice will work just as well.

If the top is browning too quickly as it cooks, cover loosely with foil.

Kugelhopf marbré au fromage et aux épinards

SAVOURY CHEESE AND SPINACH MARBLED KUGELHOPF

After buying some traditional ceramic *kugelhopf* moulds in Strasbourg (I was lucky enough to have bought two as I almost immediately broke one!), I went a little *kugelhopf* crazy. My bake-a-thon consisted of testing out an array of options, both sweet (see page 254) and savoury. This recipe uses ingredients that produce a fun pattern in the bread. Spinach lends itself well as a natural dye, giving the dough a deep green colour, as well as keeping the bread deliciously moist. The bread can be served on its own or cut into slices and eaten with cold meats and cheese. See the photographs on page 257 showing how to make this *kugelhopf*.

Serves 8

Preparation time: 45 minutes • Resting time: 6 hours, or preferably overnight • Cooking time: 45 minutes
Equipment: a 20cm kugelhopf mould or a 900g loaf tin

1 egg mixed with 2 tbsp milk • a handful of pine nut **For the normal dough:** 150g strong white bread flour, plus a little extra for dusting • 1 tsp sugar • ½ tsp salt • 3g instant dried yeast • 45ml milk • 1 egg, beaten • 35g unsalted butter, softened and cut into small cubes, plus 1 tbsp for greasing • 75g finely grated mature Comté, Cheddar or other strongly flavoured hard cheese **For the spinach dough:** 400g frozen spinach • 35g unsalted butter, softened • 1 tsp salt • ½ tsp freshly grated nutmeg • a little coarsely ground pepper, to taste • 150g strong white bread flour • 3g instant dried yeast.

First make the normal dough. Mix together all the dry ingredients in the bowl of a food processor fitted with a dough hook. Make a well in the middle and pour in the milk and egg. Mix on a medium speed for 6–8 minutes, until the dough is soft, smooth and elastic.

Add the softened butter, bit by bit, and continue to mix for about 5 minutes, until the butter is thoroughly incorporated. Add the grated cheese and continue to mix. Scrape the bowl with a spatula to ensure all the butter is mixed in.

Once a dough has formed (it should be slightly sticky), transfer it to a large clean bowl. Cover with cling film and leave in the fridge until it has doubled in size (ideally overnight).

To make the spinach dough, cook the spinach in a pot of boiling water for 10–15 minutes. Drain, and when cool enough to handle, squeeze out the excess water. You should be left with roughly 270g spinach. Stir the butter into the spinach and leave to cool. Season with salt, nutmeg and pepper.*

Mix together the flour and yeast in a bowl. Add the spinach and knead until you have a smooth ball of dough (it may be a little sticky). Place in a bowl, cover with cling film and leave the dough to rise in the fridge along with the plain dough.

Lightly dust a work surface with flour. Roll out the normal dough to form a rectangle roughly 20cm x 30cm with the long side facing you. Brush egg wash over the dough. Do the same with the spinach dough and lay it on top of the normal dough. Fold the bottom edge to the middle, and fold over the top half to meet it. Brush with egg wash and then fold the bottom half over the top half. Egg wash the ends and stick them together to form a ring – if you're using a loaf tin, skip this last step.

Grease the kugelhopf mould with the tablespoon of butter. If using a loaf tin, line it with baking paper but do not grease it. Scatter the base with the pine nuts. Place the ring of dough in the mould and brush with egg wash. If using a loaf tin, shape the dough into a sausage shape the length of the tin. Pop the dough into the tin and brush with egg wash. Cover with a clean damp tea towel or cling film and leave somewhere warm to rise to double its size.

Preheat the oven to 200°C. Brush the kugelhopf with the remaining egg wash and bake for 30 minutes or until a skewer inserted into the middle comes out clean.

Remove from oven and leave to cool for 10 minutes before turning out on to a wire rack.

Les petites astuces – tips *Over-season the spinach with nutmeg and pepper, as the flour will dilute the flavour.

If the top browns too quickly as it cooks, cover loosely with foil.

Tarte au fromage blanc

CREAM CHEESE TART

When asked to imagine a cheesecake, almost everyone thinks of the famous New York incarnation. Well, Alsace is the home of the French cheesecake, and it is by no sheer coincidence that they also happen to produce the most unctuous and creamy fromage blanc in France. Contrary to the popular belief that French food is very rich, Alsacian cheesecake is remarkably light and airy, and even lends itself to using fat-free fromage blanc (although I tend to go for 15 per cent). While the New York version relies on thick cream and cream cheese, the French cousin gets its lift from a billowy meringue base.

Serves 6–8

Preparation time: 30 minutes

Resting time: 1½ hours

Cooking time: 1¼ hours

Equipment: a 24cm springform cake tin, greased and base-lined with baking paper. Wrap a double layer of foil around the outside and the base to make it watertight.

½ quantity sweet pastry dough (see page 275)

For the filling

2 egg yolks

zest and juice of 1 lemon

1 tsp vanilla extract

150g icing sugar

40g cornflour

50g milk powder

300g fromage blanc, thick Greek yoghurt or quark

7 egg whites

First make your pastry (see page 275) then, using your hands, squash the mix into a ball. Transfer this to the prepared cake tin and use the palm of your hand and a spatula to carefully flatten it out to evenly cover the base of the tin. Prick the pastry base with a fork and chill in the fridge for 30 minutes. Preheat the oven to 180°C.

Bake the pastry base for 15 minutes or until golden, then remove from the oven and leave to cool. Meanwhile, prepare the filling. Whisk the egg yolks with the lemon zest, vanilla and half the icing sugar until thick and creamy. Beat in the cornflour and milk powder followed by the fromage blanc.

In a separate grease-free glass or metal bowl begin to whisk the egg whites with a couple of tablespoons of the remaining icing sugar. When the whites are foamy, add the lemon juice and the rest of the icing sugar, and whisk until soft peaks form. Beat one-third of the egg whites into the fromage blanc until smooth – make sure there are no lumps. Delicately fold in the rest of the egg whites.

Place the foil-wrapped cake tin in a large, deep roasting tray and pour in the mixture. Spread out with a spatula to create an even surface. Pour water into the tray to a depth of about 2cm. Carefully place in the oven and immediately lower the temperature to 120°C. Bake for an hour then leave to cool in the oven for another hour or so with the door open. Run a sharp knife around the inside edges of the tin before un-moulding the cheesecake.

Berawecka

SPICED FRUIT AND NUT LOAF

In my mind, this is the Alsacian version of the British Christmas cake; a dense loaf packed with dried fruit, nuts galore and with a hint of spice and rum. While it is jam-packed with all these marvels, unfortunately it doesn't look very attractive, so I decided to dress mine up in a little cloak in the form of a thin layer of dough. When you cut a slice from the loaf the juicy fruit-and-nut filling is revealed. I love to eat a thin slice, toasted and slathered with butter, and it works equally well as part of a cheese platter.

Makes 2 loaves

Preparation time: 20–25 minutes
Soaking time: 8–48 hours
Resting time: 3–4 hours
Cooking time: 30–35 minutes

100g finely chopped candied orange

100g dried figs, knobbly stems removed and roughly chopped

100g dried apricots, blueberries, cranberries or other dried fruit

100g raisins

2 tsp ground cinnamon

1 tsp ground ginger

100ml rum

zest and juice of 1 orange

zest of 1 lemon

150g strong white flour

150g strong wholemeal flour

7g dried instant yeast

1 tsp salt

175ml water

150g firm pears, such as Conference, cored and grated

100g walnuts, roughly chopped

1 egg mixed with 2 tbsp milk

Stage 1: Mix together the candied orange, dried fruit, spices, rum, orange zest and juice and leave to soak overnight but preferably for 2 days.

Stage 2: Sift together the flours and yeast with the salt. Make a well in the centre and pour in the water. Gradually draw in the flour from the edges and knead by hand for 10–15 minutes. If the dough feels sticky, sprinkle it with a little flour. Leave to prove in a warm place for 2–3 hours, covered with a clean damp tea towel or cling film.

Add the grated pear and walnuts to the soaked fruit. Mix together and drain off any excess liquid. Turn the dough out on to a work surface and cut into three equal parts. Return one part back to the bowl and combine it with the fruit mixture, kneading it together with your fingers. Set aside.

The two remaining pieces of dough will be used to make the outside of the loaves. Roll each piece into a rectangle (20cm x 30cm and 2mm thick). Brush with the egg wash. Place half of the fruit mixture in the middle of one sheet of dough and pat it down to form an even layer, leaving enough dough on each side to cover the filling. Fold over the sides and place on a baking tray, with the folds underneath. Repeat for the second loaf.

Brush the loaves with egg wash and prick all over with a fork. Leave to prove in a warm place for 30 minutes. Apply a second coat of egg wash and cook in the oven for 30–35 minutes at 200°C, no preheating required. The loaves should have a rich brown colour. Remove from the oven and leave to cool on a wire rack for 5 minutes.

Boules de neige à la noix de coco

COCONUT SNOWBALLS

When I visited Alsace just before Christmas, a veil of fresh snow dusted the countryside, perfect for getting that festive feeling going. These little coconut snowballs lie somewhere between a macaroon and a meringue; snow-white and puffy, like perfect little *boules de neige*.

Makes 20–24

Preparation time: 10 minutes using an electric whisk or food processor, or 30 minutes by hand

Cooking time: 1 hour

50g egg whites (roughly 2 eggs)

2 drops of lemon juice

80g sugar

a pinch of salt

150g desiccated coconut

Preheat the oven to 100°C. Line a baking tray with baking paper.

Whisk the egg whites until white and slightly thickened. Whisk in the lemon juice. Gradually sprinkle in the sugar and salt, while whisking, until stiff peaks form. Fold in the coconut.

Using two teaspoons, form small balls of the mixture and carefully drop them on to the lined baking tray. Place the tray in the oven and use a wooden spoon to wedge open the oven door slightly. Bake for an hour, or until the snowballs are dry on the outside but still slightly moist in the middle. When cooked, they should slide off the paper easily.

Remove from the baking paper and leave to cool completely on a wire rack.

Une petite astuce – tip Make sure the egg whites are opaque and have thickened slightly before incorporating the sugar, otherwise they won't form stiff peaks.

Faire en avance – get ahead The snowballs will keep in an airtight container for several weeks.

Schwowebredele

SPICED ALMOND BISCUITS

Nutty, crunchy and fragrant with plenty of sweet spices, these biscuits are definitely among my favourites, having sampled many different types of *bredele* (Christmas biscuits).

Makes approx. 40 biscuits
Preparation time: 25 minutes
Resting time: 2 hours, or overnight
Cooking time: 10 minutes
Equipment: a selection of biscuit cutters

250g plain white flour

2 tsp baking powder

125g ground almonds

zest and juice of 1 lemon

zest of 1 orange

125g confit orange, finely chopped, or 100g chunky marmalade, sifted and orange pieces chopped

2 tbsp ground cinnamon

125g butter

150g soft brown sugar

1 egg, beaten

Mix together the flour, baking powder, almonds, lemon and orange zest, the confit orange and the cinnamon. In a separate bowl beat together the butter and sugar until fluffy then add the egg followed by the lemon juice. Stir the dry ingredients into the wet ingredients and mix until fully incorporated. Chill in the fridge for 2 hours or, ideally, overnight.

Line a baking tray with baking paper. Divide the dough in half and roll between two sheets of baking paper to a thickness of 2–3mm.

Using the cutters, cut out the biscuits and place them on the lined tray, leaving a finger-width space between each one. Repeat until all the dough is used (you can re-roll any cut-offs). Chill the biscuits in the fridge while the oven is preheating to 180°C.

Bake for 10 minutes, or until the edges of the biscuits have browned. They will be slightly soft when they come out of the oven. Leave to cool on a wire rack. They will keep in an airtight container for up to a month.

Une petite astuce – tip If your dough is too soft to handle at any point when rolling, freeze it briefly.

Faire en avance – get ahead The dough freezes well. Remove from the freezer about 1 hour before rolling out.

Baking fingerle with Madame Geisert

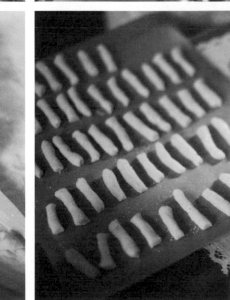

Fingerle

FINGER BISCUITS

Baking biscuits for Christmas is a longstanding tradition in the Alsace region, with many different variations all being captured under the title *bredele*. Madame Geisert, who has been baking biscuits for longer than she can remember, and now bakes them with her grandchildren, gave me a special lesson in *fingerle*. Traditionally, they are simply rolled in plain sugar to give them a crystal crust, but I like to roll mine in flavoured sugars to give them an extra twist.

Makes approx. 60
Preparation time: 20 minutes
Resting time: 1 hour
Cooking time: 10 minutes

125g unsalted butter

125g sugar, plus 6 tbsp

1 tsp vanilla extract

1 egg

250g plain white flour

1½ tsp baking powder

a pinch of salt

¼ tsp ground cinnamon

½ tsp extra fine lemon zest

Beat the butter, 125g sugar and vanilla until pale and fluffy. Crack in the egg and mix together. Add the flour, baking powder and salt and use a pastry scraper or a fork to 'chop up' the mixture until it is crumbly. Then, using your hands, bring it together to form a ball. Wrap in cling film and chill in the fridge for 1 hour.

Preheat the oven to 180°C. Line a baking tray with baking paper. Pour 2 tablespoons of sugar on to a plate. Mix another 2 tablespoons of sugar with the cinnamon and spread on to another plate. Do the same with the lemon zest and the remaining 2 tablespoons of sugar.

Split the dough into three equal parts. Take one piece and begin to roll it between your palms or on a work surface to make a long sausage, about 1cm thick. Cut the sausage into small finger length-sized pieces. Roll and lightly press each piece into one of the sugars. Repeat for the remaining pieces of dough, rolling in one of the different sugars (plain, cinnamon or lemon) and place on the lined baking tray.

Cook in the oven for 10 minutes; they should be quite pale. Remove and cool on a wire rack.

*Une petite astuce – **tip*** If the dough melts in your hands while you're making the *fingerle*, rinse your hands under cold water to cool them down – make sure you dry them thoroughly.

*Faire en avance – **get ahead*** These biscuits will keep in an airtight container for a good couple of weeks.

Make your lemon sugar a couple of days in advance and keep it in an airtight container; the flavour will be stronger.

A note on equipment

While my apartment doesn't boast the largest kitchen, I do have a decent amount of equipment I can't live without.

When it comes to baking and patisserie, precision is important and **digital scales** are a must for things like choux pastry (see page 274) and shortcrust pastry (see page 276). A set of **measuring spoons** is very useful for measuring yeast (see the brioche and kugelhopf on pages 218 and 254).

You might have noticed I use a lot of **piping bags**, disposable or otherwise. They might seem like a faff to use but actually they give a neater and more professional look to even the simplest of things, and allow you to be a little more accurate with the more fiddly details (for example, the chocolate eggs on page 215).

Muslin cloth is excellent for straining broths (like the tourin on page 70) and poaching, and can be easily machine-washed for reuse multiple times.

Microplane graters make easy work of zesting lemons and oranges, and I always have a **speed peeler** to hand for vegetable ribbons as well as peeling vegetables. A small Japanese **mandolin** slices quickly and precisely for perfect vegetable rounds (for example in the vegetable tian on page 166) and easy onion-slicing in an instant.

Digital thermometers come in very handy for making caramel (page 48) and tempering chocolate (as for the chestnut truffles on page 169).

To sterilize jars (for the marinated vegetables on page 154 and the Espelette jelly on page 127) either run them through the hottest cycle in the dishwasher or wash in soapy water, rinse well and then place, open, in a cool oven at 130°C for 15–20 minutes.

A note on ingredients

Butter I use unsalted butter unless otherwise stated. See also the note on French dairy produce, opposite.

Citrus fruit All citrus fruit, especially where the zest is used, should be unwaxed and preferably organic.

Eggs Medium, ideally organic, eggs are used in all the recipes unless specified otherwise.

Egg whites These can be stored in an airtight container in the fridge for 3–4 weeks and frozen for up to 3 months. The average weight of an egg is 55g, with the white weighing just over 25g. So if a recipe calls for 1 egg white and you have stored them together, simply measure out the white to approximately 25g using a scale.

Fish Always source MSC-certified fish and experiment with more sustainable varieties.

Gelatin My recipes use fine leaf gelatin. Gelatin leaves require soaking in cold water and then squeezing to remove excess moisture before adding to warm liquid.

Salt I use sea salt such as Maldon or *fleur de sel* for seasoning my dishes. The taste is milder than average table salt and the small investment makes a world of difference and lends a far softer finish.

Sugar Caster sugar is used in my recipes unless otherwise stated.

Vanilla pods Plump bourbon or Tahiti vanilla pods are ideal for cooking. Once you have removed the seeds, dry the pods out in a low oven and you can add them to a jar of sugar to make vanilla-infused sugar.

Yeast I use instant or fast-action dried yeast, which can be added directly to the dry ingredients in your baking, without the need to activate separately.

Some notes on French dairy produce

Living in France and having access to the best *fromageries* has certainly had an impact on how I cook. France is highly regional in its dairy consumption; while butter and cream features heavily in Normandy and Brittany, olive oil is favoured in the south.

If you are vegetarian, be sure to check if your cheese contains animal rennet.

Fromage blanc Thick, creamy fromage blanc generally has a higher fat content than fromage frais; quark is a good substitute if it's not available.

Fromage frais Fromage frais is another curd cheese. It is lower in fat than fromage blanc and it can often be substituted with Greek yoghurt.

Crème fraîche The thick French version of soured cream, available in most supermarkets and always to be found in my fridge.

Buttermilk – *Lait ribot* Buttermilk is a by-product of butter-making and it is widely used in Brittany and Normandy. Using buttermilk in cooking has many benefits, from giving pancakes a light and fluffy texture to breaking down the proteins in meat, tenderizing it. (See the buttermilk lamb on page 30.)

Basics

For the Choux Pastry

125ml water • 125ml milk • 100g butter, cut into cubes • a pinch of salt • 1 tsp sugar • 170g strong plain white flour, sifted • 4 medium eggs

Pour the water and milk into a small saucepan and add the butter, salt and sugar. Place the pan over a high heat until the butter is melted and simmering around the edges. Turn the heat to low, add all of the flour and beat hard. At this point the mixture will have the consistency of lumpy mashed potatoes. Continue beating until you have a smooth ball that pulls away from the sides of the pan without sticking.

Remove the pan from the heat and continue to beat until the dough is cool enough to touch. Mix in the eggs one at a time; the batter will be lumpy when you first add them, but beating continuously will smooth it out. Once all the eggs are incorporated and the mixture is smooth it is ready to be scraped into a piping bag.

*Les petites astuces – **tips*** Make sure the butter is completely melted in the milk and water and the liquid is simmering around the edges before you add the flour. If the mixture isn't hot enough, the starch in the flour will not be activated and the batter will not thicken.

Make sure to beat on a low heat. At first it will be a lumpy mashed-potato consistency and then a big smooth lump.

Use medium-sized eggs. If the eggs are too big, it will make your batter too runny. If you want to be super precise, 1 egg without its shell should weigh 50g.

Incorporate the eggs while the mixture is still warm but not boiling hot. If it's too cold, then the eggs will be harder to incorporate and also the batter may be runnier.

For the Shortcrust Pastry

(see Walnut and buckwheat caramel tart on page 223)

90g soft butter • 45g icing sugar • a pinch of salt • 2 egg yolks • 135g plain flour

Using a wooden spoon, beat together the butter, sugar and salt until soft and creamy. Mix in the egg yolks to make a smooth paste. Add the flour and use a pastry scraper or fork to 'chop up' the mixture until it has a sandy texture. Use your hand to gently shape into a ball and then wrap in cling film and chill in the fridge for at least an hour.

For the Sweet Pastry

(see Chocolate and crème fraîche tart on page 216 and Cream cheese tart on page 260)

120g butter, softened • 60g icing sugar • a pinch of salt • 2 egg yolks • 180g plain white flour

Using a wooden spoon, beat together the butter, icing sugar and salt until soft and creamy. Mix in the egg yolks to make a smooth paste, then add the flour. Use a pastry scraper or a fork to 'chop up' the mixture until it has a sandy texture, making sure you incorporate all the flour into the butter. Squash into a ball with your hands, wrap in cling film and chill for at least an hour.

For the Flatbreads

150g strong white bread flour, plus extra to dust • 100g wholemeal bread flour • 1 tsp instant dried yeast • ½ tsp salt • 1 tsp sugar • 115ml warm water • 1 tbsp olive oil • 4 shallots, peeled, halved and finely sliced • 2 heaped tbsp finely chopped herbs (a mixture of parsley, dill and chives works well)

Tip the flours, yeast, salt and sugar into a large bowl. Add the warm water and oil and bring together with your hands. Knead intensively for 10 minutes, or, ideally, use the dough hook on a food processor. Add the shallots and herbs and bring the mixture together to form a smooth dough. Place in a bowl and cover with a clean damp tea towel or cling film and leave in a warm place for 1 hour.

For the Pizza Dough

250g plain white flour, plus extra for dusting • 1 tsp salt • 7g dried instant yeast • 60ml olive oil • 150ml warm water

Mix together the flour, salt and yeast in a large bowl. Make a well in the centre and pour in the olive oil and water. Mix together to incorporate and then turn out on to a floured surface and knead until the dough is smooth and elastic. Return the dough to the bowl and leave to rest at room temperature for 30 minutes.

For the *Béchamel Sauce*

30g butter • 30g plain white flour • 500ml lukewarm milk • ¼ of an onion, peeled • 1 clove • 1 bay leaf • a pinch of grated nutmeg • salt and white pepper

Melt the butter in a large saucepan over a medium heat. Add the flour and beat hard with a wooden spoon to a smooth paste. Remove from the heat and gradually add a quarter of the milk, beating all the time. Switch to a whisk and add the rest of the milk a little at a time.

Place the pan back over a medium heat, add the onion, clove and bay leaf and simmer for 10 minutes. Whisk frequently or it will catch on the bottom of the pan. If the sauce becomes too thick (it should be like thick custard), whisk in a little more milk. Remove and discard the onion, clove and bay leaf, then add the nutmeg and season with salt and pepper. Pour the Béchamel into a bowl and cover with a layer of cling film touching the surface (to prevent a skin from forming). Place in the fridge and to leave to cool.

For the *Mayonnaise*

2 egg yolks • 1 clove of garlic, peeled and crushed • 300ml sunflower oil • lemon juice, to taste • sea salt

To make mayonnaise, place the egg yolks and garlic in a large glass or non-reactive metal bowl set on a damp tea towel (to stop the bowl from slipping). Whisk the egg yolks a little, then add the sunflower oil drop by drop until the eggs begin to thicken and become pale in colour. Continue drizzling in the oil until you have achieved the consistency you like. Add lemon juice and sea salt to taste.

Une petite astuce – tip If you have a food processor, blitz the egg yolks and the garlic, then gradually add the oil until you achieve the right consistency.

For the *Praline*

50g blanched skinless hazelnuts • 75g sugar • 2 tbsp water

Line a baking tray with baking paper. Toast the hazelnuts in a dry saucepan until they are golden. Remove from the pan and set aside. Put the sugar and water in the pan and heat gently until the sugar dissolves. Increase the heat to high (avoid the temptation to stir it). When the caramel begins to turn a dark golden brown, remove from the heat and quickly stir in the hazelnuts. Pour immediately on to the lined baking tray and spread out evenly. Leave to cool. Once the caramel is cool and hard, blitz to a fine powder in a food processor.

Index

Page numbers for photographs are in **bold**

Remerciements

Writing a book and certainly a cookbook is not an easy feat. It is not a simple act of sitting down and typing away on the computer. This book started with me getting on a train, plane and other modes of transport to visit, meet and learn new things about the different food traditions around France. The inspiration for these recipes would not have been possible without the help of the many people I met along the way (some of the pictured and written about in the book). To all the producers, bakers, cooks, farmers and passionate food people (Michaela Spielvogel at Slow Food France), un *GRAND merci*!

Back in the kitchen it was my trusty two ring gas hob, toy sized oven and my friends who were there giving me feedback on the concoctions I created. Thanks for being great guinea pigs guys!

Special thank you to Lindsey Evans and the whole team at Penguin for being encouraging, supportive and excited about my new adventures beyond my little Paris kitchen.

Cher John Hamilton, *Merci beaucoup* for all your hard work and enthusiasm for this book. Your attention to detail has made it special.

Chère Lizzy Kremer, You're the best literary agent one could wish for. Your support and the team at David Higham has helped me to grow as a food writer.

Cher David Loftus, As always you make my food (and me) look beautiful, regardless of the weather or late night. And BIG thank you for putting up with my 'love of speed' in the car.

Chère Nathalie Redard, Thank you for searching the lengths and breadths of France to find the perfect plate, fork or other prop paraphernalia. It has certainly paid off because the dishes look fantastic!

Chère Frankie Unsworth, *Merci mille fois* for traipsing in the rain, mud and getting lost in the French countryside with me. Your hard work has helped me make this book the best it can be. I couldn't have done it without you!

Chèrs my loving family and Robert Wiktorin, Thank you for being there and putting up with me no matter my mood.

Many thanks to all the people who helped out on the photoshoots around France: Marie Constantinesco, Amie Brennan, Sarah McLoughlin, Amélie Riberolle. Véronique Daudin at Ecolodge des Chartrons, Aurélien Crosato, Madame and Monsieur Constaninesco, Jean-Luc Colonna, Daniel Rozensztroch, Régis Godon, Elisabeth Simon, Marianne Ménard. Catherine Madani, Genevieve Goux, Anne Cardot, Hélène de Bettignie, Laurence Lagrange, Papier Tigre, Myriam Balay Devidal, Gabrielle Franck, Émilie Mazeaud, Nathalie and Christophe Hurtault, Marjorie Goaoc, Elodie Rambaud, Bachelier Antiquités.

And the shops and brands for lending us some beautiful props:

MERCI
www.merci-merci.com

BACHELIER ANTIQUITES
www.bachelier-antiquites.com

ASTIER DE VILLATTE
www.astierdevillatte.com

MEMENTO
www.facebook.com/MementoBrocante

ARTOCARPUS
www.facebook.com/galerieartocarpus

COPIRATES
http://lescopirates.fr

PIED DE POULE
http://www.pieddepoule.com

STAUB
http://www.staub.fr

LES GUIMARDS
http://www.lesguimards.com/lesguimards.com

MUD
http://www.mudaustralia.com

LE GARDE MANGER
https://www.facebook.com/pages/Le-Garde-Manger-Aligre-Paris-12%C3%A8me/106656756022428

LE PRÉ AUX CLAIRS
http://www.lepreauxclairs.com

LA COLLINE
https://www.facebook.com/pages/La-Colline/273845949372350

Merci beaucoup, à bientôt